Even in Death
Love Pursues Us

Linda L. Baldwin

DORRANCE
PUBLISHING CO
EST. 1920
PITTSBURGH, PENNSYLVANIA 15238

Dorrance Publishing Co
585 Alpha Drive
Pittsburgh, PA 15238
Visit our website at *www.dorrancebookstore.com*

ISBN: 978-1-4809-8272-7
eISBN: 978-1-4809-8247-5

Prologue

Dedicated to anyone grieving over life itself!

In today's computerized, technical, and impersonal world, it could be out of date to write a story about a love that never dies.

The two main characters in this true story shared a love that didn't end with the male character's death. Even in Death goes beyond the experience the two characters shared while both lived their real lives on earth. They begin to learn – one dead, the other alive – through the help of their family and friends, that what we can't see forms the basis of what we can see. Sounds like a simple formula for living a joyful life, but the characters in this story share the equal task of finding true happiness. We see that the characters, including the two soul mates, must take time to listen to life and how their lives connect to true meaning, even when they must take chances to find that connection.

They learn that we avoid the reality of death like the plague, not thinking that it could lead to true meaning of life and not sure if that's all there is to life or if life continues after death.

Most scientists like Carl Sagan have decided upon evidence they culled from the material world that there probably isn't an afterlife. Even great minds can't say for certain that life doesn't continue after death. The characters in this story are ready to change their minds and say there is life even in death.

No one can say with absolute certainty that life ends with death. This story wants there to be life even in death with every word written and uttered in the pages of this story. The path the characters in this story take is as if they are conducting an experiment, one of love, probably God's love.

We have all agreed that we can't see love, but that it exists. Theologians believe that force is God in action. Scientists aren't sure what it is but they see stunning evidence that something has timed life to an absolute degree or life as we know it wouldn't exist at all.

The author of this story believes that the only way you can prove that there is life even in death is through the power of love and faith combined. Call that force something else if you will, but it appears that if we let love have its way, it will lead us to our truest fulfillment while we live on this planet and after we leave it. It is imperative that we make the decision for love and not give the opposing forces power to destroy life. Al-Shabaab, an extremist group, entered Carissa University in Kenya, separated out the Muslims, and slaughtered one hundred and forty-seven Christian students.

Love is a neutral but positive force that is greater than the evil forces that are currently causing chaos in the world. Love never segregates or judges. It says this and more about love in 1 Corinthians 13, found in the New Testament.

If we don't make the decision for a love that can't be destroyed by death, there will be more senseless killings until more and more people, maybe all people, forget that love was created to save our souls. The two main characters in this book grow to realize this with the help of each other even though one of them is dead by earthly standards. It's not that the author advocates disregarding earthly standards, some of them have served us well and gotten us this far in our evolutionary development.

Sadly, we are on the verge of parting ways with the force of love we believe represents a God we think we no longer need or want or believe exists. This story wants to give people a chance to reclaim a belief in an eternal love that rescues us from our harshest, most awful selves before we destroy ourselves and the planet.

This story affirms we can't reach our destination beyond total destruction and be freed of our baser side without God and love guiding our way. When we surrender to God's love, we will understand that death has never been our enemy but has tried to spare us from instead surrendering to those baser drives that are endeavoring to make deep, negative inroads into what we consider civilized life.

Thank you for reading this important book.

Author: Linda L. Baldwin
Date: April 3, 2015

Chapter 1

Life Starts with Death

March 2015 - There are so many wars waged in the world that experts have lost count. Wars in the past involved five percent non-combatants, today they involve seventy-five percent of non-combatants.

March 23, 1775 – Patrick Henry ignited the American Revolution with a speech before the Virginia convention in Richmond stating, "I know not what course others may take, but as for me, give me liberty, or give me death!"

He was back in her life, this time dead on the earthly plane. Come, now, she didn't expect life and death to work together like this. Oh, unless you were living beyond the three ordinary dimensions that regulate our lives. I may have slipped into the eleventh dimension.

Isabel Louise Cappston, everyone called her Louise, Joe called her Izzy, had lived in the fold of many spaceless and timeless dimensions before she met Ted forty-some years ago when she was young and foolish. He was Ted Jacob Silva-Ventura, a man who had loved her with his whole heart, mind, and soul but she had been afraid to take his love into her soul. She couldn't tell anyone how she knew he was back in her life though he had been dead for eight years! She knew she would learn how the more she opened up to the possibility. He was back to claim her soul with no evidence that could prove he was alive on the earthly plane. No one would condemn her for ignoring his entrance into her life.

When her cell phone played Beethoven's Ninth, she glanced at Jessie Ferguson's name,

"What's on your mind, Jessie?"

"Do you remember where we were forty-three years ago? We've been friends a long time," Jessie reminded her.

"Yes, we were finding an apartment for you in Houston after you divorced Larry. What a pleasant divorce compared to mine."

"Do you remember that guy you met when we were eating our supper in the dining room of that fancy motel we couldn't afford? Your napkin slipped off your lap as you got up from the table as if you planned it. He reached it before you did."

Chills ran up and down her spine. *Was this a sign that he's back? What on earth made you think of him?* This was too much of a coincidence for Jessie to mention him now when she hadn't brought up his name in years, not since Houston in the early seventies.

"What was his name, Ted something or other?"

"I think you're not from this planet, Jessie. How on earth did you know he's been on my mind?"

His name triggered memories of that time in her life when love was scarce and she was convinced no one could ever love her in this lifetime. Stan, her ex, had said she was inferior to him and incapable of being loved. "No man in his right mind would want you, Louise," he told her this often, so she believed him. When they divorced, he changed his wording to, "no one will ever find you worthwhile or appealing".

Ted loved her in ways that she could not forget no matter how hard she tried. He told her, through his probing green eyes and his gentle words, "We are one". He had appreciated every particle of her being that was united to his without any effort on her part.

On this March day, after a winter piled high with snow, she thought she heard his voice and felt his vibrations. She knew they did not come from a sex-starved human male. It had been his way of alerting her before he called her. She could only think he was trying to contact her today.

"Jessie, I don't know how to tell you this, you'll think I'm crazy, but he's back on my wavelength."

"Did he call you, you know, on the phone then?"

"Jessie, he's dead. He died eight years ago. He's come back! Don't ask me how. I can't see his face but in my mind I see his green, penetrating eyes, not like any eyes I've seen on anyone I know on earth. When she told Jessie the details of what she had felt with him, she tingled from her solar plexus into the rest of her being. "Jessie, I'm tingling like he's ringing my built-in phone."

"Louise, what kind of friend would I be if I didn't tell you to answer his call? I know how he made you feel when you were with him. No one has ever made me feel like you were a nova exploding all over the place."

"I'm a supernova that is exploding from the Big Bang, only the source isn't alive by our standards. What do you think he wants?"

"Oh Jessie, I'm so sorry he's back to confuse your life. You were just getting settled."

"Life is confusing until you find your way. You know that better than most people I know, Jessie."

"All I know is that marital love dies quickly. This love Ted has come back to claim hasn't died. What does this say about marriage?"

"It's true Jessie, marriage as we know it is in trouble. If we could be married to our soul mate, the marriage would last forever. I've discovered that kind of love doesn't die with death. It's an 'either or' situation. People who are married in their spirits will remain together in their spirits for all eternity or, if they are not wedded in spirit, the marriage can't last. I think this is true, but it hurts to admit it. Some of us have been too immature to grow up in our spirits in time to save our marriages."

"Louise, are you saying a soul mate serves a different purpose than a marriage-mate?"

She was thinking aloud when she answered Jessie's question, "If he's my soul mate, and I think he is, then he's come back into my life, even in death, to help me do something difficult. It might be possible that it hasn't happened yet. He's bailed me out of difficult situations before in another lifetime. Good marriage-mates often do this for each other. My grandparents are a good example."

"This is beyond my comprehension, Louise, but I can see you believe what you're saying. If only we could be married to our soul mates, if we could ever find one. Oh, hey Louise, sounds like you're sure he's back for some reason. I guess I'd be concerned what it is."

"According to my vision, it had to be in another lifetime, he came in on a ray of light... No, wait, he was clad in light. I watched him crash land into a bramble bush, thorns and all."

"Landing in the middle of a bramble bush had to hurt. You told me the vision was from a previous life when you were a nun. You haven't changed much, have you Louise?"

Louise had retired last month from thirty years as an interim minister who was a conflict resolver in her particular denomination. "Some things never change, as much as we would want them to. Yes, I was a nun in an order that had made my life miserable. excuse me, we make our own lives miserable. I still don't know if this is totally true." She went on, remembering the vision. "I wanted to leave but didn't have the means. One day, when I was outside the convent, standing on a hill where the garden was that I was ordered to hoe, I saw this light brighter than the sun speed towards me. I thought it was a sign from God that I had disobeyed. Without hesitating, I fell to the ground face down and hoped God would forgive me. The light did not make a loud noise as it streamed over my motionless body, I thought that was strange. The light disappeared as if it had not existed, I thought that was even stranger. But who was I? I was no light expert. There were only candles in the convent."

Jessie hadn't heard this part of the vision. "Louise, wasn't this soul mate of yours hurt when he crashed landed into that bramble bush?"

"I peeked up from my prone position on the ground to see if I could find the source of the crash. It came from that confounded bramble bush I had often fallen into when I was ordered to walk and pray, walk and pray, until I tripped. The bush wouldn't burn to help me find my way. When I crept nearer to the bush, I heard curses and a thrashing commotion before I saw him emerge, disheveled and bloody. He carried his shoe in one hand and with the other he was picking off the thorns from his head. He asked me if I had a rag or anything he could use to wipe off the blood that was dripping into his eyes from his forehead. I took the hem of my ugly black robe and wiped off the blood."

"Louise, did he see you before you wiped the blood from his eyes and forehead?"

"He looked me square in my eyes and said, 'Oh, it's you, glad to see you'. My mouth dropped open at the same moment he dropped his shoe. 'Ouch,' I remember he said, 'ouch' again. Then he laughed the loudest laugh I had ever heard. I looked up to see if it rattled the convent windows. I hoped it had."

"That light-clad man with the scraped forehead and lost shoe, he's Ted, the man you and I met in Houston forty-three years ago. Right, Louise?"

"I said that! I must be losing my mind. Yes, I think the light I thought had disappeared was him clad in light, I thought was a strange outfit from any world."

Jessie asked her, "What happened next? You never told me all the details of this unusual vision."

"He wrapped me in his light and we streamed away, clad like two melded wires. My God, the first fiber optics able to combine us into a stronger unit and travel without interference or static from Mother Superior who was running toward me shaking her fists. We were gone from that hill before she could ruin the connection."

A song played in her mind as she remembered what he had taught her when they were flying through space on his streaming ray of light that kept them safe.

"Life is love, life is energy, and I'm forever even without the mind I know. The person I was, I am. I am he, he is me, and we are part of everything, everywhere. How successful are we. Moreover, the love that put us together as one is the only action worth our time."

She was searching for a tune she thought he had hummed on that journey they took together. She calculated was back in the fourteenth century. If she saw him again, she'd have to ask him to hum it again. Beethoven's Ninth tune? Why not!

He said she had to overcome her fear of love and life. He had come for her on that hill overlooking an ocean, maybe in Portugal, where she was a nun in an ancient, awful convent. Her future was bleak and dark until he freed her with the rays of his optimal way of communicating in that dark time.

"Jessie, it's his mission in his cosmic life to rescue me from difficult if not impossible circumstances. What does that say about me? No one else I know has to always be rescued from their clumsy self. I am always falling into bramble bushes."

"What's so impossible about your circumstances now?" Jessie Ferguson was a Jew by birth and had converted to Christianity because of Louise and her strong faith. She wasn't afraid to ask questions that might make it easier for Louise to answer Ted's call, dead or alive. *Love is love,* Jessie thought, *it doesn't have to depend on your state of being, does it?*

Jessie had a natural beauty, one that make-up artists couldn't paste or dab on, nor would she have let them. Her skin was dewy fresh. Her eyes were the color of the sky and her hair smelled pure, free of harsh shampoo chemicals. Consequently, she was the best friend in the world because of her pure, firm, and most loyal intentions. She was the best person Louise knew except for her father, who had taught Louise how to discern the difference between good and evil. Jessie didn't have an evil bone in her body and Louise knew she could trust her with this supreme example of absurdity.

"Louise, you know that I'll never betray you like some of the people in our lives have betrayed both of us".

"Okay, I know it's time to move on. How, Jessie, do I move on with a dead person?"

"Find out what he wants. Maybe we don't know enough about death. Maybe death isn't death and is something we haven't defined or experienced. Say what?"

"This search goes against everything I have believed with my whole heart, soul, and mind and have encouraged others to believe about faith, love, life, death, and God. I feel like I am abandoning my faith."

"Louise!" Jessie was bouncing up and down with excitement. "Maybe we're about to make a breakthrough onto another level of existence that's getting ready to emerge the way your soul mate emerged from that bramble bush. Your faith won't crumble. It's too strong."

"Yes, but…"

"Not this time, Louise, this time don't interrupt with sensibility, that ingredient that has boxed you in from the Dark Ages until today."

"You sound like Ted, that's what he would say to me. I'm too wrapped up in this mortal coil. It tries to cuddle and entice me into its folds and make me believe it's time for me to die. I'll die and that's all there will be. Poof, I'll be gone forever!" She spit out the last four words into empty space.

"Isabel Louise, Izzy... Do I sound like your mother? What are you saying? Has your faith been as empty as the space you spit into?"

Louise's words had changed Jessie's mind about God and how important she was to God. She was determined not to let Louise lose her faith and become a slobbering fool.

"Where are you hiding, Ted? Come out. Come out of your bramble bush please," Louise whimpered. At least she didn't slobber like a newborn, too long without love and attention. She wanted to gather in every morsel of the love and attention she had given others like someone who hadn't eaten in days or centuries. Jessie told her to wait a while longer. Be patient. As heaven was her witness, patience was not one of Louise's virtues.

"You look famished. Can I prepare your favorite sandwich, a BLT without bacon? I'll add slices of avocado instead. A BAT? While I'm slicing and slathering, tell me about Grandma Isabel. What's happening with her?"

"And Grandpa Jim, the only two people I know who have a love that will outlast death."

Chapter 2

We Grew up Along the Way

March 25, 2015 – A German commercial plane crashes, killing 150 in the French Alps with all nationalities aboard, including two infants, sixteen teenagers, and two teachers.

March 25, 1911 – A raging fire erupted inside a garment factory in New York City killing 148 young women employed as low-paid seamstresses. About fifty of the victims had jumped to their deaths from the eighth floor rather than perish from the flames. These mostly immigrant women, who worked six to seven hours a day in cramped, dangerous conditions, earned about $5 a week.

March 25, 1807 – The British Parliament abolished the slave trade following the long campaign against it by Quakers and others.

After Louise had said goodbye to Jessie, she recharged her cell phone. Their hour catch-up time helped them recharge their lives so they could navigate the curves ahead. Louise thought how life is a journey and that some roads lead to success and happiness while others lead to dead-ends and bitterness. Her mind skipped to Ted and how he and they grew up apart from each other. They had no idea who the other was when they traveled the sidewalks, backyards, alleys, and streets of the towns where they grew up to be the people they are today, one living, the other dead.

There were no cell phones, iPhones, internet, Twitter, Facebook, or the other instant ways of communicating that this month, March 2015, made her yearn to live in that simpler, less invasive time.

Ted was more street-wise than she was. She took for granted how safe and secure she was living close to farm land and her farmer relatives. If they didn't farm themselves, they owned farms they employed others to till, reap the harvest, and thankfully provided well for her family. When my father's father, Grandfather Jim, tried to convince my dad to move to and operate one of his farms, Dad said he couldn't. After the twinkle and easy smile disappeared from his face, Grandpa Jim heard him say, Frances, his wife and my mother, would never agree to leave their home in town.

My father was never happy after he gave up farming with his bare hands the way his mom and dad had. His mother Isabel had suffered from Alzheimer's and was recovering from it, much to everyone's amazement but not to Grandpa Jim. The doctor tried to tell him that this is only temporary, don't count on a full recovery. Grandpa Jim had told the doctors not to discount Grandma's Isabel's strong will. "She will fully recover in spite of your prognosis," he told the physician in charge of his wife's care.

As for my father, he was forced to give in to his strong-willed wife, my mother, and was never happy using his rational powers after that to make a living for the family. Grandpa Jim watched him struggle with his thorny issue until he died. Grandpa thought that was his way to escape the dilemma presented by my mother's determination not to compromise. She didn't expect it would make him that unhappy. Louise hoped this was true.

Ted's parents lived on a ranch outside Reno, Nevada where they raised cattle, horses, and grew their own fruits and vegetables. He learned how to be street-wise when they moved to a second home in the city where Ted and his brother went to high school. He learned he wasn't as tough as the rest of the guys who said they were his friends. He had a softer side that appreciated the words people did not say and glances they shielded from public scrutiny.

Ted's mother told him he knew what she was thinking before she opened her mouth to speak. He didn't take her seriously, though he did wonder why he knew what he knew when he knew it and how he came to know what and who spoke to him.

Louise never thought twice about hearing people speak without moving their mouths. She always knew who would call before the phone rang. She thought what she could do with her mind was normal. She never told anyone she had this normal ability. If she were street-wise, it came from a world whose streets and ways didn't exist in the world she could see.

Ted wanted to learn how to communicate better in a world where he observed no one listened to what was being said. He promised to some unseen force he'd listen to more than he spoke. After that, he was amazed he could hear what people weren't saying. He wondered why he was given this special gift as he called it. There are worlds out there that we can't see but that exist right next to us. Is that where our loved ones go when they die? When Ted thought about the dead members of his family he missed, he said to himself, *I hope I will see them someday.*

Louise lost her father when she was the unhappiest in her life. Her marriage had failed. Stan, her ex, was cold and uncaring. He didn't marry her because he had loved her. He said they could have smart kids together, like the Aryan race. She wanted to take back the love she continued to feel for him but found she couldn't.

Louise believed and taught others that there are many different loves we experience, some die, most change, and very few never die, even in death. Her love for Stan had morphed into the realization that he had never loved her. She couldn't help it. Her love for him would never die on the earthly plane. She didn't want it to continue even in death. The pain they inflicted on each other surely wouldn't follow them beyond death. She had a lot to learn about death.

A prime example of a love that would never die is the love she had for her twin sons, Kevin and Kurt. She loved them so much she would die for them. At the very least, she would do everything she could to keep them and their families safe from harm and needless suffering.

The love she had for her father didn't die with him. It increased the more she felt unloved by Stan. How is it that your husband who promised to love you "until death do us part" betrayed that promise seconds after it was made? Her father had tried to help her answer that question the month before he died. She did not believe any amount of love would heal the wounds from Stan's betrayal. He found someone else to love. Her father had tried to reassure her that she was lovable, she'd find someone to love her one day. "You will see," were three of his last words.

"Oh Dad, why'd you leave me?" Her anguish and pain were so intense because she couldn't see him, talk to him, or touch him. She knew he wouldn't walk up the stairs into the house and hear him say, "I'm home!" When you're dead, you're dead. The body decays like a leaf. The spirit resurrects into another realm, a place we can't see with our physical eyes or prove exists. She had dual feelings about life and death. There was no doubt her marriage died a painful death without Stan's attempts to resuscitate it. He didn't want to divorce her. He wanted her to take the blame for their bad marriage and even more horrible divorce.

Her father was right. She found true love five years later when she married her second husband, Bruce, who loved every ounce of who she was. He hadn't tried to change her then disagree with the change as Stan had. She wanted to ask her father why was it that when they were the happiest, he was diagnosed with cancer and died a year later. When Bruce took his last breath, she saw his spirit resurrect like a puff of smoke rising up from remnants of burning leaves on a late October afternoon. She heard his voice tell her, "Don't worry about death. It's good, Louise". Then he was gone with a huge smile on his pain-free face as he moved out of range and left her forever. He was full of joy not of this earth. His body was shiny-new as he went on to another life. She was happy that he had successfully made the transition from this life to the next but she had to work at forgiving him for leaving her.

While all these memories were flooding her mind, she remembered Clara, a ninety-three year old member of one of her churches she sat with as she was dying. Clara was like her grandmother, Isabel, who loved her with no conditions as she grew up. Grandma Isabel was a love that would never die. Clara, a virtual stranger, had become a love for Louise that would never die. While Clara was dying, before she took her last breath, a smile widened by inches across her face and her eyes brightened with a light that was not of this world. Louise thought she must be seeing someone she knows, her husband who had died fifty years ago or Jesus whom she had loved all her life. Both loves had given Clara a strong faith that had kept her family together through tough times. Louise could see with her own eyes that life continued even in death. People who believed this unverified truth, like Clara's daughter, didn't talk about it with others.

When Louise thought about her grandmother, Isabel, and Clara's struggles with life and death issues and how they had remained loving and kind, she felt better about life and her place in it. She, herself, had helped many people find their way in life as they stumbled and fell over insurmountable obstacles. Others, like Grandmother Isabel and Clara, could see beyond limitations that discouraged people from finding true love. These two women were Louise's guides even in death. *This is great,* she thought, *how the living and the dead give us reason to go on living.*

She thought about how successful her twin sons Kevin and Kurt and their families were. She took great satisfaction in knowing she made the right decision when she told Ted she couldn't leave her family for the love they had found in Houston forty-three years ago. She could see she was a good person who had integrity and worth and courage, the qualities Stan told her she didn't have a week after they were married. Bruce made sure, before he died, that she knew how special and worthwhile she was. "Don't forget you need to do what you do best. Go be a minister!" And she did! She went to seminary and became a minister in her denomination in part because Bruce had affirmed her purpose in life. *Someone has to believe in you*, she thought while Beethoven's Ninth played its lovely, otherworldly, and powerful tune on her cell phone.

"Didn't we just talk?" Louise asked her friend Jessie.

"That was yesterday. Are you losing track of time, Louise? No matter, I have the question of the twenty-first century."

"I can see some things never change. You have a dramatic streak that has forced me to think beyond my morasses. What is it?" She scratched her nose, which told her someone was going to visit her soon, if you believe in that old adage.

"What makes you think he, Ted, is back in your life?"

"Strange you should ask. I was cleaning out my storage room when I found several boxes of pictures of my great grandparents, grandparents, parents, my children, and my grandchildren. You know me. I sorted through every single picture…"

"You came across those letters from Ted you thought you threw away years ago. Am I right?"

"You're spooky, Jessie. How on earth or heaven do you know that? Forget I asked that question. The letters were in among the pictures."

"Well, is that why you've started to think he's back?"

"Gee, Jessie, the letters were taped back together again. I remember I ripped them up and thought I threw them away."

"You definitely threw away some of them, I saw you do it. You must have saved one or two of his letters at the last minute."

"Whatever the reason is that I saved them, I have this feeling he is trying to tell me something only I don't know what it is. Do you?"

"Are you kidding me? How would I have any idea how this other level of existence works. I'm planted on earth like that elm tree that used to be in your parents' backyard."

"It was split down the middle by a tornado that ripped through town in the early fall. No offense to you, it's hard to lose something you thought would outlive you. You, on the other hand, underrate yourself, Jessie. You are like a diamond with many facets that catches the light. You have the ability to see beyond the ordinary and unnecessary things in life."

"What does that mean? You're straying." Jessie wanted an answer.

"How about this, there's more to life than we can see."

"Are you saying that along the way we learn we can love many different people and that some of them may not love us back?" Jessie cringed at the thought, but knew it was true.

"Some of those, shall we say, well-meaning people will love you back in ways that will test your resolve and deplete your inner resources." Louise saw the light turn on in Jessie's whole being.

"And cause us to grow up," Jessie concluded.

Louise pondered in her heart how we grow up along the way. We never attain our full potential, she was not sure of that. Life is a journey, someone said, not a destination. Jessie and she had made great progress along this particular part of the journey. They could both say that many questions don't have answers – yet. Then she remembered her grandparents and how much they were still influencing her progress and she was grateful!

March 26, 2015 – The Lufthansa co-pilot delib-
erately flew the plane into a mountain in the
French Alps. That crash killed 149 innocent souls.
No one knows why Andreas Lubitz did something so horrible.

Chapter 3

Proof that He's Back

Thursday March 26, 2015 – Yemen overthrown by Iran-backed Houthi Rebels. U.S. troops evacuate.

March 26, 1970 – The Camp David Accord ended thirty years of warfare between Israel and Egypt. Prime Minister Menachem Begin of Israel and Egyptian President Anwar Sadat signed the treaty of mutual recognition and peace fostered by U.S. President Jimmy Carter.

March 26, 1992 – The Soviet Union (USSR) collapsed and became the Commonwealth of Independent States.

Louise had retired from her thirty-year career as a conflict resolver and interim minister in her particular denomination. She was eager to begin a new venture that hadn't come to her yet. She missed the people she had nurtured and the conflicts she had helped resolve, but not enough to want to return to a church and people stuck in their own bramble bushes or conflicts with or without their shoes on or their spirits intact.

Suddenly, like a lightning bolt, the vision came to her of Ted flying toward her on a comet, later she knew it was his own light. The light quietly zoomed over her head while she lay paralyzed with fear face down on a steep, craggy hill by that awful dark, dank convent she knew existed somewhere in a time she couldn't place.

After his body crashed landed in the thickest, deepest part of the convent bramble bush, not a burning bush, and before he could rescue Louise, he had to find his shoes. She heard him cursing and thrashing about in the bush as she walked nearer.

"Ouch, damn, forgive me, Lord!" He emerged bloody and exhausted with one shoe dangling in his hand. "Where in hell, that bush is hell, is my other shoe!" He sat down hard on the ground and tried to put on his shoe.

"Do you need help? I see you found your way out of this maze of a bush. That's a great accomplishment, maybe a miracle." For the first time in her boring life, Louise, the nun in a convent along the coast in some nameless country in perhaps the fourteenth century was fascinated by his appearance. She thought he might be handsome if she could see his eyes. They could be blue-green but blood from the thorns was dripping into them from his forehead. "Here, let me wipe the blood from your eyes." She did it with the hem of her garment.

He didn't move a muscle, except for his mouth. "I'm here to help you get out of this thorny situation. Of all things, the helper has become the helped."

It was easy for her to find the right path to his other shoe while avoiding the thorniest of the thorns. "Who are you?" she asked, as she dropped his other shoe in his lap.

He said his name was not important only, "I am 'The One Sent to Free You'!"

"Free me? Me, free? What's free?"

Before he rose to his feet, he had explained how God was not the mastermind behind her plight. "We subject ourselves to endless, meaningless, and boring routines in order to teach ourselves when we are ready to move on to another level of life. You cannot blame your decisions on Mother Superior, as committed as she is to making you conform." He didn't prolong describing her innate powers of perception and operation when he saw a strong beam of light radiate out from her inner core and heal all her wounds.

His agreement with her that God could heal all old wounds gave them the energy to be suddenly lifted up and away from her self-inflicted lifestyle that had imprisoned her soul. *Zip, boom, bang,* they were out of sight before Mother Superior could grab her arm and force her down to earth. They could hear her raised voice, "You must immediately get back to your necessary routines! Only they will save your soul!"

She noticed that the light clad them both in its regal, shiny splendor. The first fiber optics! He was brilliant to be able to design it so it would provide an unbreakable connection from them to the energy source that, with their agreement, had pulled them, not pushed them beyond conflict into a true peace dimension.

Her faith began to make more sense to her in that split-second lift off than it ever had while she prayed spread-eagle upon a floor she had just scrubbed cleaner than clean. She didn't have to work hard to accept the nature of this faith that was freely given to her along that fiber light connection. She sang a song to herself, "I was a slave to my faith and didn't enjoy it the way I am now, lighter than light, brighter than bright. My faith will sustain me forever."

In the future, she vowed she'd be a wiser steward of the life-force she could never own or be able to sell. Her soul mate taught her that she'd only be able to share it or give it away to others who were living in worse circumstances than hers.

The first fiber optics expert was her soul mate, the great communicator who shared his skills with her before he died the normal way we think people die. Something told her there is more to dying than taking your last breath. She was sure you were never ever disconnected from that fiber connection to the light source she called love. We are always clad in the light that protects us from losing the identity God gives us in the beginning of time. Yes, that's it. He's alive on that light connection that transported us into another dimension not available to the person who has normal expectations of dying. That old concept might be getting ready to change or catch-up with what is the truth about living, dying, and the light she wanted to call love.

Ted, her soul mate, the great communicator-traveler, was asking me to rescue him? Had he fallen off his light beam? Ted had come to her rescue to remind her she had a light beam of her own.

While she was assessing her abilities to rescue someone she thought was dead, she heard him talk to her in her mind, "No, you are perfectly capable of removing others from dilemmas they've created and helping them turn on their lights. You've had plenty of experience turning on your light in the darkest places and finding your way. It's hard to deny you've not seen the light when you have."

Was that Ted? Is he talking to me? Sounds like something he would say

"Learn to believe in yourself and your light," he'd tell her. "Don't think less of yourself. You can do anything you set your mind on doing. Don't forget that." And she had until now.

Her father had tried to remind her not to forget who she was, a torchbearer he had called her. Dad had this mystical way of transmitting power to her without trying. He didn't harp at her to get her act together or else, like some parents would. He told her he knew there was much more to life than we can see with the naked eye. He told her this as if it were the biggest secret in the universe. His voice orchestrated his words in the most firm but tender way, giving vent to his soul's desire to compose a heavenly symphony. She was in awe of his unspoken belief in a power source that he could not verify by material standards. He had passed the torch to her that night they stood leaning up against the porch railing, gazing up into a clear star-filled night. He didn't need to tell her the mysteries of life, light, and love. She heard it in his voice and saw it in how he adored life itself. She murmured to herself that fathers are so important to the well-being and happiness of their daughters.

She came back to earth with a gentle bounce and landed in her library where all her treasures were from relatives living and dead. She saw her mom's antique desk she had put in the opposite end of the library where she used it to showcase other family keepsakes such as her father's pictures of the family, his paperweight with pennies frozen in plastic space, his old traveling man made out of Ecuadorean wood he had bought at an auction. It was standing in front of the desk.

Her mind was talking to Ted, her soul mate of centuries ago. "If you're alive, though you be dead, give me a sign I can see with my own two eyes." She had pushed against the limits of a dimension she couldn't see, touch, or feel and she shuddered inside.

Louise, people called her Izzy, had no way of proving he was alive though dead, unless Ted would suddenly appear in the room where she stood groping and reaching, trying to touch something or someone she couldn't see as if she were blind.

Where she stood in her library, she was surrounded by two thousand books on shelves built into the wall in back of a second desk that was hand-crafted for her brother sixty years ago when he was a kid. On it sat a globe she had retrieved from the trash after one of her friends, Joe, had thrown it away. She was sure it was Joe who thought she didn't need an old globe, that she could order the newest globe on Amazon.

Her mind was tired of trying to contact a dead guy, soul mate or not. She had a thought frame of Joe, Joseph Franklin Firoved or Frankie, her colleague in ministry, crop up suddenly in her mind range. She replayed a conversation they had had a week ago about their growing up experience in their hometown south of Naperville, Illinois where they currently lived and worked their careers. He calls her Izzy. She liked to be called Louise.

"I know everyone calls you Louise but I think you're an Izzy, not Isabel or Louise but Izzy."

"How about Louie for Louise?" She had suggested this name in the conversation she was replaying as if Joe were in the room with her.

"No, Izzy, you're an Izzy!"

"That sounds so nervous. I'm not a nervous person. Did you know that my grandmother's name is Isabel? Did you know she is recovering from Alzheimer's disease that all her doctors considered impossible? She's the least nervous person I know."

It was as if Joe had not heard her news. "My grandfather's name was Frank Joseph. Quite a switch, aren't I, from the normal Frank?"

"You are extraordinary with unusual insights into death and dying people and how you've been able to be a hospice expert for twenty years, almost without a break, Joe. You've watched more people than you can count die painful, agonizing deaths! How have you done it?"

"I grew tired of coming up with inspiring sermons and watching some of my flock show me their watches while I was preaching or draw their hand across their throat. One lady jingle-jangled her keys then dropped them on the un-cushioned pew with a clatter. That's how they told me it was time to end my sermon."

"Is that the reason you ended your preaching career? You resigned a week later. I didn't know the reason. You never told me. How awful, Joe. Working with dying people is more rewarding. They are eternally grateful, I've discovered."

As she was having a mind-conversation with him, the door bell rang. No need to wait for her to answer, he banged on the door. She opened the door. Joe was ready to bang again.

"Frankie, put your fist down, I'm here. I've been thinking about you. Great minds work together. Weird! Have you ever heard anyone tell you that one of their loved ones who had died came back into their lives?"

"What in the world possesses you to ask that question? Are you going to ask me to come in?"

"When you're deep in thought, you lose your manners."

"Okay, mother! Right words are hard to find to describe something that makes no sense to me. I'll ask this way: have you ever heard of a dead guy communicating with someone as if that dead person had come back to life? That's the best I can do. It sounds impossible, doesn't it to you?"

"You're testing the limits, Louise. Who is this dead one who has come back for, who, you, Louise, Louie, oops, Izzy, you? You look like you've seen a ghost."

"Can you help me find proof that this person is not dead in the coffin/grave state of dead?

"Hmmm, a mystery for Sherlock. How are you going to solve it?" He was the cutest boy in her class when they were kids. Nothing defeated him. That is, until his father died when he was a freshman in high school when he needed him the most. After that, he grew sullen, studious, lost his cute edges, and committed himself to a goal he didn't share with her.

"I don't know, Frankie. You have to help me without accusing me of being a detective. You knew I wanted to be a detective when we were exploring the neighborhood and back trails as kids."

"Not a problem. Now that you know that I'm not judging you, give me more information so I can get to work on this mystery...Sherlock. Just call me Watson."

"Stop calling me Sherlock. Just call me a death, not a dead, detective who is convinced that this person, who has been dead eight years has come back into my life. I need to, no I have to, be able to see him so I can rescue him."

"Any clues? Is there a reason to think you haven't lost your mind and all this is coming from your over-active imagination and, oh, your need to be loved?"

"Thanks. No, I deserve your words. I found letters I thought

I had torn up and thrown away years ago from this man I met... Do I have to go into the details of how we fell in love? I found them when I was cleaning out my storage room."

"I'm impressed with your efforts and your love for a stranger. I only see you as upright, uptight and a true conformist. No way would you violate the way your mother taught you how to eat your soup."

"Ouch, that hurt, but it's true. I found his letters taped back together and I can't remember tearing them up or why I saved them. Maybe a phantom saved them. The letters made me think of this person that has been absent from my mind for decades. I've been too busy helping God save churches. He had slipped into a dusty file in the back of my mind."

"Is that my destiny? I'll slip into that dusty file and never be found again. Maybe that's how he feels if he's back from the dead. He has come to claim his file before it's too late."

"I think he's going to ask me to help him repair his light. Why should I try?"

"You love him and it's not a common, ordinary love."

"Go on, tell me how I fell in love." There was a smile flickering on her face, but her eyes were deadly serious as they stared into his. His smile faded quickly.

"How in the hell, sorry, do I know?"

"We've been friends all our lives, that's why!"

"What's his name, can I ask that?" He was on the verge of smirking but covered it with a serene smile. He was aware that this issue was major and could change her whole life.

"Ted Jonathan, no, Jacob, Silva-Ventura."

"He's not from, excuse me, Ted is not from around here. He comes from a long line of people who gave him riches most of us don't possess."

"Where did you get all that?"

"I'm the real Sherlock. You only played being a detective when we were trying to solve a mystery when we were kids. Remember those secret trails we blazed? Every kid in the neighborhood tried to discover our trails. When they did, we'd blaze others. Then they'd find those and we'd blaze others ad infinitum until we looked for other mysteries. This one is a lulu!"

She then knew Joe's willingness was a sign that Ted had come back for her. Frank's insights came from a source outside his reasoning abilities that he valued highly, so did she. He wouldn't admit to her he had intuitive powers.

"Izzy, I don't know where I'm getting this information. Maybe he's come back. I'm just saying maybe he has. Don't get too excited or worried yet."

They were both exhausted from thinking beyond the dimension where they had functioned with their senses cocked and ready to go help others on a minute's notice. It was much easier to function on the dimension they could see, the one they called God's kingdom. They talked about how they could see proof of how it worked in the lives of the people they had helped survive horrible situations. What gave them great satisfaction was when someone they had guided through a traumatic event immediately helped some struggling soul make it through theirs. They were able to reason that if a God they couldn't see could provide guides exactly when needed to perform a miracle then an ordinary dead guy could come back to ask a favor.

"Izzy, if you and I disappear from the face of the earth one day, I'll hold you responsible for making me use my powers. Before that happens, I hope you come rescue me."

"You're saying you'll watch my back like you did when we were fighting our way through grade school? Nothing could be rougher or tougher. By the way, I'm always watching your back."

"I'm here for you too. You can count on me. I hope I'll learn more than I did in grade school. I was never so glad to get out of that jungle in my life."

"Until your father died."

"Wait, tell me how your Grandmother Isabel is. Did you say she is recovering from Alzheimer's? I must have misheard you. No one recovers from that disease."

Proof of life conquering death is everywhere, but we can't or won't see. Joe knew she was thinking that her soul mate was alive. He had overcome death!

Chapter 4

Different Intentions, Same Outcome. We're Going Home!

March 27, 2015 – Still trying to determine why the Lufthansa plane crashed in the French Alps. It's hard to realize the co-pilot did it on purpose.

March 27, 1977 – The worst accident in the history of civil aviation occurred as two Boeing 747 jets collided on the ground in the Canary Islands, resulting in 570 deaths. The Canary Islands are located in the Atlantic Ocean near Morocco and Western Sahara, both in Africa. You might have heard of Tenerife?

When Joe opened the door of Louise's townhome to leave, his eyes were big as saucers, "Am I helping you because I've never accepted my father's death? I thought I was beyond denial and grief." He knew he could never quit missing his father. He was befuddled by his own mental condition as he walked out the door and onto the sidewalk that led to Louise's driveway where he had parked his car in front of her garage.

"You need to put air in your tires. They look low to me," one of her passions in life was to sell cars and she did when she was between church jobs.

"You know me Izzy, a car's a car. I'll drive it until it falls apart."

"Right, I know, but it will cost you less if you maintain it properly… Forgive me. I don't mean to lecture you." Louise was trying to retread his thoughts so he wouldn't skid on them.

"You're preaching to the choir. I'll take the car to the station on the corner and have air put in my tires."

"You could do it yourself, you know."

"And change my own oil like you do on your days off?"

"Now I have every day off. I could completely redo my engine while I'm at it."

"Speaking of your days off," he was saying this as he got into his car with his head resting on the top of the car. "When do you intend to get your proverbial ass in gear and find something else to do? Oh excuse me, we are going to look for a dead guy. That should take, I don't know, a few months at most before we get discouraged and rethink our idea about death."

"Get out of here, Frankie. I'll call you when I need you." She was laughing to herself when she walked into her home she loved. Before she closed the door, she took a deep breath and thanked God for her friends. "What would I do without them," she cooed to herself.

She didn't plan to preach to herself when she said we all have different intentions in life but we somehow or other reach the same outcome. What that means, she'd find out. What she didn't know is how soon she'd arrive at an outcome she didn't expect, a new home.

"Who said that? If you're here Ted, reveal yourself. Tell me you're not dead and how you're not dead. Why you're here?"

No answer. She was beginning to equate his silence to the four hundred years of no word from God between the Old Testament and New Testament times. Where was God? Had God disappeared from the face of the earth and found refuge in the outer edges of the cosmos? Does God exist? Maybe God took a vacation. How far is it to the outer edge of the cosmos? She wished Carl Sagan were still alive, he'd know. Probably billions and billions and billions of light years, he only ever said billions once in reference to the cosmos and its activity.

Or, she answered herself by asking, was it because we human beings have turned a deaf ear to the idea of a God who cares about us even if we are billions of miles from this God who cares? She reasoned that miles or light years didn't make a difference to God and in that quick second of time, she declared she didn't feel cut off from God. Others, she was sure, wouldn't think in a billionth-of-a-second interval when it came to their faith.

What bothered her more than the existence of God is the destination of the spiritual essence of the self. She believed the spiritual being never died. What happened to it after death? Did it go be with God and live at God's left hand since Jesus was living on God's right hand? Or did it float around in outer space seeking a good place to dwell?

Her theology was tired and worn out. It needed a major readjustment that would happen, without much effort on her part, as she searched for Ted, the dead love of her life. She called him instead her soul mate. Her friends believed that the term soul mate existed in fairy tales and didn't exist in real life. She believed her grandparents were soul mates. She persisted in calling Ted her soul mate. We all have a soul mate. She had read somewhere that you rarely, if ever, marry your soul mate, except for her grandparents. Why would you want to ruin a good thing? Although her grandparents had a marriage straight from God's heart. She was just getting in good with God since she made the decision to quit the ministry. Better stated, she had taken a vacation from God as God was coming back from taking a vacation from the human race.

What are my intentions now and what outcome can I expect? Shall I sell cars? Shall I knit until my fingers fall off? Her mother had taught her, with some degree of frustration on her part, how to knit when she was a child barely able to hold the knitting needles. *Shall I work part-time with people who need guidance in the spiritual area of their lives?*

When her cell phone rang, she heard Joe tell her not to think too much and to get on with her day. How did he know? Oh, sure, some people are born on a different wavelength. Joe was one of those sensitive souls.

"What are your intentions Joe and what outcome do you expect? You're one in-tune guy. How'd you know I was stuck in creeper gear and not anxious to shift my gears?"

"I'll get back to you another day. For now, I know I have to help you find your center again. In that way, I am becoming convinced the farther I drive from your house, the closer I get to my center."

They both lived and worked in the suburb of Naperville, Illinois, about thirty miles from Chicago. Their families had come from central Illinois, where their hearts and roots remained planted in the richest farmland in the world. Joe didn't like the volume of traffic and longed to live in peace and solitude where he could get right with nature. He took trees, grass, the land, and creatures that inhabited all three for granted as if they had been created for him, not he for their protection. He was beginning to dislike the fact that human beings, himself included, were being so careless with the world's resources.

Louise needed to find this dead love of her life. Joe was beginning to aim for the same outcome. In the process, he might be able to let go of the idea that he'd see his father one day. He'd been hanging onto that idea the day they put his father into the ground. He was a freshman in high school and couldn't accept the image of him lying dead in the coffin, forever underground. Everything about his father was gone, obliterated in one moment of death like the crash of that airplane into the side of a mountain in France. Gone, nothing left. Not even a whisper of longing.

Is that really true? When Jesus died and then was resurrected, was God telling us that one part of us lives on, though only a select few have ever wanted to believe that? *Or,* he thought as he drove through a part of town where there wasn't as much traffic, *is it our intention to keep our loved ones close to us forever and we'll hang onto them any way we can? Death negotiator, would you come back…if?* He didn't know what he meant, but he believed Louise was going to find her dead soul mate, dead by earth's standards, and that he was going to help her. How, he had no idea, but he was sure they'd have to have God's help. *This is a desperate situation,* Joe reported to himself. *Along the way, I believe I'll find my father in excellent shape. We will have to pray with a kind of desperation Hannah had when she prayed for a son. Then Samuel came into being and he changed the world.* "This might work," he exclaimed with a renewed spirit that arose in him. "Hey, I missed my turn!"

Louise didn't know enough about the outcome of her quest to be hopeful. Joe reached hope before she did when he turned onto the street to his apartment. Her mind was spinning in circles objecting to the upcoming change in direction. She was a creature of habit, the very best of the nesters. The more she settled into her home, the more she didn't want to leave it and the deeper she kneaded the nest, like a cat would who had not been properly weaned from its mother.

"I can wait until tomorrow to start my search for Ted." Refrains of *Gone with The Wind* and Scarlett O'Hara's last statement when Rhett Butler stormed out of their mansion elicited a strange response from her, *that's not me, never has been, never will be. So there!* What she didn't know is that Joe wasn't going to leave her in her quandary, neither would Jessie. Both their futures depended on how well Louise explored hers.

Her special insight for the day was we are all dependent on each other. We don't do anything alone or without hurting or helping others. She thought again about the deadly crash of the plane into the French mountains and how one person's decision impacted the lives of not just one hundred and forty-nine others but countless others who had depended on them for love and friendship. She would "get her act together," a term her mother had laughed at when Louise had said it to her. She probably understood that Louise would rather rehearse scenes the rest of her life.

We all have the same outcome, she thought as she got into bed, turned out the light, and left on the T.V., things were happening so fast in the world, she didn't want to miss any major event. Her last conscious thought was of the co-pilot's act of violence against not only his family but to the whole universe. He had planned how he would take a shortcut home and he didn't seem to mind that he was taking a plane-load of innocent people with him. Her soul mate would not present this alternative. She was sure he would not lure them into a numbing, crushing, dangerous, and, in the end, futile outcome.

In her dreams, she played among the stars with her soul mate and her idea of what love really is. She saw colors she had never seen on earth and wondered if ever there would be a day when human senses would return to their original brilliance. The dream ended at dawn when she awoke with the realization that the love from God that some people shared with their soul mates is always brilliant, free of rough edges that wouldn't inflict unnecessary violence on unsuspecting souls.

Chapter 5

After the Age of Innocence

Human beings must purposely take time to discern where they are going or they spin out of control. The image of her father teaching her how not to spin her wheels on ice popped up in the middle of this thought. She was grateful that he had taken time to teach her how to be a careful driver in a car and with her life.

Louise overslept. The birds chirping in the trees outside her window triggered memories of her bedroom window in her childhood home. There in the three tree branches that grew towards her window, birds' chirps had awakened her before her mother's voice yelled up from downstairs. "Louise, you'd better be getting out of bed now or you'll be late for school. I have an errand for you to run." She had not been Cinderella in her mother's mind, but there were times the story was appropriate.

She was transported to the good old days, where she could pause to rethink her life in peace. She saw that her innocence was cushioned in mounds of fresh qualities that had shrunk to one-quarter of their original size. She had extracted her hopes and dreams years ago and absentmindedly filed them away in the back of her mind. She'd have to become familiar with her filing system. *Tomorrow, I'll do it tomorrow. Gone with the Wind* was one of her favorite books, and Scarlett O'Hara, a strong-willed female character, gave her solace though not with the degree of the non-committal attitude she had. When she had finished her morning swim, she praised God for the beauty of the universe and then called Jessie with her renewed levels of hope and energy.

"Have lunch with me. Or we could hop on my jet and leave our baggage and cares behind. We could be in the South of France for an afternoon swim and light supper."

"Have you gone crazy? Wait, that sounds like a splendid idea. I'll get my swimsuit. I can travel light with the best of them and I'll meet you at the airport."

"No, my driver will pick you up. I wish, Jessie, it were that easy. I'm afraid there's too much sadness in that part of the world after the awful plane crash." She had come to her senses with a speed that caused her to have agonizing bends in her heart and soul. One day all the tears and sorrow will cease. The part of her brain where her faith began was tingling, absorbing, and acting alive like the energy source that had ignited the Big Bang. The intense desire to be fed by that energy source spread to her soul where it caught fire. No one today expected their soul to catch fire.

"Louise, oh Louise, are you still there?"

"Oh, my dear, yes, I am. Sorry. My mind was on the way to the South of France where I had found a beach away from all the pain and suffering."

Jessie knew her friend well. She was not insulted. "I'm afraid there is no such place in this world."

"I'll meet you at A Better Place to Eat. We'll eat the freshest salad and one half of a creative sandwich (the sandwich of the day) on toasted whole wheat bread."

When souls are starving, people stuff their bodies with food and they become obese. It was Jessie's plan to stuff hers with food free of harsh chemicals and the least amount of fat. She was far from fat and so was Louise, but they enjoyed the taste of fresh food nonetheless.

"My plan is to enjoy eating with you. I'll savor every bite of food and the tiniest morsels of our conversation. I might add a scoop of vanilla Haagen Dazs ice cream to sweeten my disposition."

"What comes next, Louise, I mean after your scoop of ice cream?" She could sense a difference in Louise. Her eyes sparkled and her skin glowed. Each word bounced out of her onto the curvy road to a new town they'd never visited, not even in their wildest dreams.

"Not sure, but I think God is communicating with me again, correction, I'm communicating with God again."

"Do you think that has to come first before you make contact with Ted?" Jessie had no idea what she was talking about, except that she had anticipated what Louise would say.

"I've never done anything major in my life without God's input first. If I try to make contact with Ted, who knows what evil force will come along with me?" Chills running up and down her spine played a strange melody that forced her to ponder what could be dangerous consequences.

"Those s-shaped curves can take us by surprise. Just so you know."

She didn't know she was on the brink of discovering how dangerous it would be if she threw herself with total abandonment into the arms of a man who had been dead for eight years. *Would he have arms? Oh, wait, would he have a body? I must know more about death.* A key purpose in her life was to stay free of unwanted influences. She told Jessie that Joe had promised he'd use his skills to keep dark forces from creeping up on her. Joe's unspoken purpose was to watch her back like he did when they were kids fighting the school bullies. His and Jessie's influence were well-documented and safe.

"I'm there for you, too. You know me, I'm pretty tough."

She took a boxer's stance, raised her dukes, and started punching the air. Truth is, apart from all the funny gestures, Jessie wanted to know more about death. Her mother, Helen had died when Jessie was thirteen years old after a sudden illness no doctor could diagnose. She was still grieving for her mother when she thought no one was looking.

It's tough to understand death in a country like the U.S. that denies death and the pain it causes. Every effort is made to keep a 'stiff upper lip'. Her father had told her that was how she could hide her grief. She held back the tears until her lips quivered, her limbs shook, and her sorrow took over every one of her actions. She was the youngest person in her class to develop an ulcer after her grandfather died, not Isabel's husband, her mother's father.

"I'm far from the innocent person I was when Mom was alive and we were each other's best friend. Oh, how I miss her." It felt good for Jessie to confess her sorrow.

"Is that the reason you are joining the search?"

"Yes, mom was, I'll call her, my soul mate. I can't get use to her absence in my life. I think I must be hopeless."

"Has this loss caused you to lose your innocence or could you say your innocence has aged?"

"I don't know the difference unless we can say love from our loved ones helps us weather storms we couldn't survive without them beside us. I have not done well without my mother beside me." Jessie knew she would never stop missing her mother.

"You've done very well. You've been the best friend in the world. I can give witness to your ability to walk beside me when the storms have raged. Your mother would be proud. She's still walking beside you."

"I want to see her, touch her, hug her, sit down with her, and have a cup of tea with those good chocolate chip cookies she'd make. Remember?"

"You bet I do. They were my favorite comfort food of all time. She made them big, thick, and cake-like, not chewy or too crispy."

Louise ministered to Jessie and watched her be restored through her own resources, that inner spirit we all have. Like a newborn baby, her soul was stretching out into the north, east, south, and west. Radiating outward, circling around, and meeting in the middle, she could feel a new age of innocence hug and dance with both of them. Love must include everyone, unless some tortured soul wants to be excluded from that radiating circle of love. If we only knew what was ahead, we would never walk or dance alone into that circle of love. Louise hugged Jessie outside the restaurant. When she did, a wave of fear tried to divert her resolve to stay hugged and secure in what she had called God's love.

She could feel rising waters of hope crumble her reluctance to allow love to move her toward her destiny. She wanted what was left of her innocence to protect her and to shelter her from the fear of love and loving. What she didn't know is that God's idea of innocence was age-old and proven by the limitless qualities of love and how it changes us in profound and sometimes frightening ways to become wiser in our innocence. Louise was thinking that love is innocent yet not naïve. It removes barriers in the way of the purifying aspects of love that make us able to perceive with wisdom and truth, not react with unjust actions.

Why did Ted leave though it appears he didn't leave? Does he want love to purify him in ways that death could not? What is my part in how love plays out in all our lives? What happens to my innocence? Louise asked this unseen force, that she hoped was love, to protect and surround her. *Will I lose my innocence or will it be strengthened and work to purify me also? After the age of innocence is not accurate,* Louise thought as she turned out the lamp by her bed. *We are learning how to love more, not less. As we do, we will keep our innocence at all cost.*

As she fell into a deep sleep she heard, she wanted to suppose was Ted say, "Trust me."

On some level, she could hear herself say, "Do I have a say in whether or not I want to trust you?"

Chapter 6

Everyone Fears Death

People were dying all over the world in wars, in plane crashes, and by natural and unnatural causes. The only way out of life was by a painful death. What a dead-end solution. Louise knew that the idea of dying had made many people so fearful they retreated into a shell or crashed a plane into a mountain with one hundred and forty-nine innocent souls aboard.

Next week is Holy Week, Louise told herself. All the cells in her body came alive but didn't know what to do next. She didn't need to prepare worship services or preach sermons, those days were in the past. She could discover the true meaning of Easter without being pressured to help others find their way out of their fear of death. Jesus didn't fear death. Others feared death for him. *What if*, she found it difficult to express this thought, *we are the ones who are keeping Jesus alive through his resurrection and the way we worship him. There, now, I've said it. You can strike me dead, Lord, right here, on the spot where I'm standing.*

She was looking out the window into her backyard scanning all her blooming fruit trees. Life wants to be life and not death no matter what human beings think about life and death. In the end, a serpentine way of thinking led to an s-curve up ahead. Up a steep incline and over our fear, like climbing Mt. Everest, we humans must know that life can't be defeated by death. If there were no resurrection, life wouldn't be filled with joy or sorrow. Louise saw robots instead of humans if they couldn't make that climb with their faith in tow.

Beethoven's Ninth played on her phone, an excellent, well-executed accompaniment to her thinking. She didn't recognize the caller from a town north and west of San Francisco.

"Who is this?" She was perplexed and anxious, only her friends had her number.

"My father's name was Ted. My name is Jacob Silva-Ventura."

Louise was so shocked she couldn't speak. Her body turned cold as ice and she shook with a rattle. It must have been her words rattling like ice cubes in her mouth.

"Are you there? Please answer. I have something important to ask you," he said. His voice sounded like Ted's.

His warmth thawed her words that streamed from her soul now warmer by the sound of his voice. "I'm here," she said. She wanted to sound strong and alert, but she was meek and humbled by the call. "Can I help you?" Each letter stumbled from words to a complete thought.

"I found your name and number in my father's things when I was cleaning out his storage area. It was in a box with your name on it. I have not opened it and I will not, of course. Dad wanted you to have it. I wonder if we could meet sometime or if I could send the box to you?" He was stronger than she was, the same kind of strength Ted had when she had lost her resolve to take their love and thaw with it.

"Let me think," she couldn't. If he were anything like his father he'd give her time.

"Take your time. I know my call has to come as a complete surprise. The idea to call you came out of the blue, like Dad was telling me to call you. I was going to put the box into a safety deposit box in our bank if I couldn't reach you."

She couldn't resist asking the next questions. "Tell me about yourself. Do you have time? If you can, tell me about the last few years of your father's life. How did he die? Was he in pain?"

"Are you asking because you also are feeling my father's presence?" That took courage, he was usually shy about asking intrusive questions.

"I am speechless, Jacob. Wasn't that your father's middle name, Jacob?"

"Yes, it was. Dad was an unusual man. I dislike saying this, but I wish I had learned more from him when he was alive. It seems I'm about to learn what I need to know from you through him."

"How did he die, Jacob? Was it peaceful? I know how your brother died. He didn't take his life, did he?" She was prompting him, but then she stayed quiet, the quietest she'd ever been in her life. This was a life and death answer.

"He didn't die peacefully. He wasn't in pain. No, he didn't take his own life, thank God. There was something he wanted me to know. I heard him whisper your name when no one else was around, right before he died."

Louise was stunned. He had never forgotten. His last thoughts were of her.

"He was a great father to us and a wonderful husband to our mother. There was never a more perfect gentleman in the world than my father. I loved him very much and want to know who you are and why his last thoughts were about you."

"I am beside myself with joy that you love your father so much and that he didn't suffer before he died. I want to tell you the whole story but I can't do it now. Can we talk later? "

"I'll be in Chicago on business next week. I took over my father's business before he died."

"That's Holy Week. You're doing business during Holy Week?" She didn't know why she asked that question.

"Yes, it's urgent business. I have to satisfy one of our most important clients, Holy Week or not."

"Where can we meet? You undoubtedly know Chicago well."

"Let's meet at the art museum, my father's favorite place in Chicago. I'll be flying into Midway in the family jet."

"Tell me when and I'll meet you at the art museum, I love the place. Before you go, tell me, was your father ill a long time before he died?"

"He was perfectly well. That's what is so weird about his death. It was as if he had an appointment he had to keep and he could only keep it if he left his body behind."

Louise was flabbergasted, "Oh my God!"

"Tell me, are you okay? I don't want this call to upset you too much."

He had his father's kindness. "I'm not fine but I'm okay, if that makes sense. I'll see you next Tuesday at the art museum, 2:00 p.m.

"One more thing, were you in love with my father? I'm sure he loved you. I know it was a good kind of love that helped him become a better person. I hope this doesn't upset you, I think he always wanted to be with you. I'm not sure why I'm so sure of that."

"If it won't upset you, I believe I can answer that question when we see each other. Love has many different ways of loving those who need it the most. We, your father and I, needed a love that would help us bridge gaps that were too wide." That answer was obscure even for her.

"Were those gaps ever bridged by your love?"

"Not while we had families who needed us," she told him. "One more thing," she couldn't hang up, "I think your father is trying to communicate with me. He's been dead eight years, right?"

This time he was the one who said, "Oh my God, yes!"

"Let's see how we can help each other, okay Jacob? I'll look forward to meeting you. God go with you and keep you safe."

"Dad use to say that to me all the time, especially after my older brother left us."

"I'm so sorry Jacob, but not sorry you contacted me. Many things will be explained."

"By my Dad, I think? Just so you know, Dad wasn't afraid to die."

"Not if he didn't die," Louise had the last word.

There are no last words when it comes to love and the course it will take even in the most peculiar of circumstances. Louise was trying to remember her last words to Ted before she didn't hear from him until now. "I'm sorry this is happening to you," she said after he told her about his son's premature death. She wondered what were some of the last words people spoke before they died. Would they indicate there is an afterlife with their loved ones waiting for them?

1) James Polk, President of the United States, uttered these last words in 1849 before he died, "I love you, Sarah. For all eternity, I love you." They were spoken to his living wife who was with him when he died.

2) Henry Ward Beecher on March 8, 1887 spoke these last words before he died, "Now comes the mystery."

3) Napoleon Bonaparte, French Emperor, spoke these last words before he died on May 5, 1821, "Josephine". She had died on May, 29, 1814. She was his wife, the Empress, and love of his life.

4) Humphrey Bogart's last words when he died January 14, 1951 were, "I should never have switched from scotch to martinis." He never lost his sense of humor.

5). Jimmy Stewart, when he died in July 2, 1997 said these last words, "I'm going to be with Gloria now." His beloved wife had died three years earlier.

6). Steve Jobs co-founder, chairman, and CEO of Apple Inc said these last words on October 5, 2011, "Oh, wow! Oh, wow! Oh, wow!"

Who or what, Louise wondered, *did he see or experience?* Maybe this great modern day inventor saw loved ones in paradise. Louise opened her Bible to the last two verses of the Book of Revelation: "He who testifies to these things says, 'Yes, I am coming soon', Amen, Come Lord Jesus. The grace of the Lord Jesus be with God's people. Amen."

Louise would be careful what she said and thought from now on, for they truly might be her last words spoken or thought on this earthly plane.

One of her favorite authors, C.S. Lewis, wrote these last words in his book *Mere Christianity:*

> "The principle runs through all life from top to bottom. Give up yourself and you will find your real self. Lose your life and you will save it. Submit to death, death of your ambitions and favourite wishes every day and death of your whole body in the end, submit with every fibre of your being, and you will find eternal life. Keep back nothing. Nothing that you have not given away will ever be really yours. Nothing in you that has not died will ever be raised from the dead. Look for yourself, and you will find in the long run only hatred, loneliness, despair, rage, ruin, and decay. But look for Christ and you will find Him, and with Him everything else thrown in." (pg. 190).

Louise assumed that C.S. Lewis meant that when he wrote the last sentence of this quote that when you find Christ and he becomes part of your life, in reality you become part of his life, then all the negative aspects of your life will be consumed by the opposite aspects. For example love instead of hate, fullness instead of loneliness, joy instead of despair, calm instead of rage, and newness instead of ruin and decay. In searching for loved ones who have died, it is then we learn how to fear death? The answer she received was that we fear the loss of love more than we fear death.

The Ninth playing startled her out of her reverie. It was Jessie.

"I just thought of something, Louise, what if we don't really fear death but fear losing the love of our loved ones when they die? All I can think about is how much I miss my mother, but more exactly how much I miss her love for me, the amount of love she showed me, how much she made me feel loved and wanted." Louise could hear Jessie's voice quiver and her breaths were short.

Such synchronicity, Louise was thinking before she said, "I was thinking the same thing, Jessie! I shouldn't be surprised that great minds work along the same lines, but I am. Yes, to answer your question, I do believe we fear losing love more than we fear losing our lives to death. Meaning that we can die while we're in our bodies as a way to prevent facing the hard facts of life like not being loved enough or at all."

This could be a great revelation that they just made together on the spiritual plane, proving that there is a spiritual or invisible plane where most thoughts, ideas, and pre-actions are formed. While they were talking on their phones, Louise noticed Joe's number flashed on her screen.

"Jessie, Joe is trying to call me. Do you suppose he has come to the same conclusion we have, that we fear losing love more than we fear death?"

"Hang on, I'll see if I can answer his call and not lose you."

"Louise, I just had this brilliant thought, when I was thinking about how much I miss my father's love..."

"I know, we fear losing love more than we fear death, am I right?"

Joe was dumbfounded, but admitted he shouldn't have been. "This is getting downright spooky that we three should be thinking the same brilliant thought at the same time while being in different places."

"Let's assume, rightly or wrongly, that there is no fear of death, okay?" Louise began. "If that is true then we might be able to posit that there is no death, just a terrible fear of not being loved enough to keep the lights on."

The three of them laughed with total abandon as a way to relieve the pressure that had been building up over the past two weeks before and after Jacob called.

"What do we do about this, you two?" Jessie asked in her usual way of wanting an answer immediately.

"I think there are people who die because they are tired of looking for love or people who have never been loved in their lives like we three have been. In that way, the body wears out in ways the bodies of people who are well-loved don't."

"Then what was Jesus trying to tell us when he allowed his body to be crucified?"

There was a collective gasp.

"Joe, that is an excellent question. What do you think?"

Jessie answered first. "Could it have been a way to show us that love is the answer to the pain we inflict on each other and the desire we have consequently to give up and die out of sheer frustration from having to look for love?"

Joe added, "You mean it was a way to express how much pain we feel when we aren't loved in the right way, by God's love, and that if we aren't too much pain results, enough pain to make us wish for death to come."

"Which means," Louise added, "that if we all were loved the way God loves us there would be no need to plan to end our lives because we think love has run out or will run out."

"We are good, aren't we?" Jessie said. "Hey you guys, Louise, I mean, what does this mean where your soul mate is concerned? Why did he bring on his own death?"

"I can't answer that for sure, except to say the death of his first son and how he took his life, took the loving nature out of him. It could have been his way of replenishing himself through dying, if that makes sense."

"Well…deep subject," Joe exhaled. "Death could put us in touch with the greatest source of love and replenishment in the universe. Maybe he needed his batteries recharged and will be back or is working on building up his reserves. The reason he contacted you is a way to confirm to himself that love is greater than death and discouragement."

"You see, you two great friends, you all have the ability to think outside the box and outside that old conventional way of thinking."

"There is no fear of death. There is only fear of not being loved," said by all three together.

Joe added, "I remember my father's last words, 'Don't forget to mow the yard this week, Joe.' I would have preferred to hear 'I love you,' now that we are talking about how important love is to our will to live. He was always concerned about getting things done and making sure we kept our lists current."

Jessie thought for a moment and said, "I don't mean to make you feel bad, Joe, but my mother's last words were 'I love you, Jessie. Don't forget that I'll love you forever.' I promptly forgot that she tried to fill me full of love and began to feel sorry for myself until this very minute when I suddenly remembered her last words."

"My father told me to get him something to take away his pain, 'Get me something, Louise,' and I thought he meant he wanted me to help him end his life. Bruce, my husband who died, his last words were, 'I love you'. I know that some people don't say anything. Clara, the lady in my first congregation, smiled this huge smile that covered the universe in its scope then died. It was as if she saw someone who loved her and she loved, which proves that what we need most is love, that bright, indestructible light that can't be destroyed by death."

"Wow, do we have a lot to learn about love and death and living between these two forces," Joe had the last word.

Chapter 7

Now What Will We Do?

After Jacob said goodbye, Louise invited both Jessie and Joe to dinner that night. She needed to nurture their bodies as she probed, not use, their hearts and minds. She wanted to ask them what to do next now that the search was broadening.

"Saint Joseph and Mary, Louise, did you in a million years expect this kind of thing to happen?" Joe was as shocked as she was.

"Is this the way the dead come back to life, through their children?" she asked Joe.

"We may have unleashed some primeval force. The sins of the father... Please start to pray for God's guidance and protection. You're better at praying than I am." He was acting like a coward, but underneath he was anxious to face the challenge.

They talked and planned and laughed and cried until 8:30 p.m. when Joe started to leave.

"Wait a minute, are we agreeing that Ted is alive and is here with us, only we can't see him?" Joe was asking the right question as the death expert.

"We have to ask God to lead the way here or we might find ourselves at a dead end, no pun intended." Louise had a sense of humor that could save the day on down the perilous road.

"Let's agree to stay together in our spirits while we go through Holy Week and you meet Ted's son, Jacob. Do you think he'll bring along his father? Kidding, just kidding. Don't hit me." Jessie was ready to have fun, too.

"You know something, Jessie and Joe? I think this is going to have a happy ending. If we can have a sense of humor about death, what does this say about the future of death? Can we change the mind of a person scared to death of dying?"

"I wouldn't go that far, Louise. It's hard enough to die. To die with a sense of humor is asking too much," Joe was shaking his head and wondering if there is such a thing as death.

Louise beat him to the idea, "What if death is an illusion? We only think we die."

'This is getting too unusual and weird for me and I'm one of the weirdest and most unusual people I know." Jessie got up from the table, walked around the living room, stretched her legs, and extended her arms over her head to bring back the blood to her brain. She sat down with a plop and a heavy sigh of relief. "There now, I'm ready to tackle anything that comes our way."

"I'd pour some wine but I don't drink and neither do the rest of you." They weren't against drinking. They didn't want to take any chances that the wine would distort their thinking.

What they were about to think next was way too important to drown the thought in a glass of wine.

"Do you believe that God planned it this way, Louise, that we would think we were going to die, have us go through the process of dying, then change the direction of our exit?"

"Jessie, your thinking is always direct, without complicated nuances. There are no s-curves in your future. Yes, I think we're on to something by George."

"Speaking of George…" George was her silky-black male cat's name. He was around someplace in her townhome, no doubt curled up down under all her pillows piled high on her bed where no one would find him. He was an alpha cat who ran the house with an iron paw. Nothing could be out of place or he would knock it over with a loud bang or thud that would startle her.

"You know, George Oscar has been acting stranger than usual. He looks up and around him like someone is in the room. His eyes get saucer-like, his black coat shines brighter in the dark, and he runs for cover in among my pillows." She named him after her grandfather she had missed since he died when she was in high school. He had a massive wave of silver white hair and lived next to a castle on an island off the British Isles before his mom and dad moved them to the U.S. He filled her imagination with who his play mates were and what the other side of him was like. She was sure George's sparkly black coat did not represent a dark side in her grandfather.

"Do you think George sees what we can't, a spirit whose name is Ted?" Joe said this as he moved to the edge of his chair. His funny side had been replaced by the side of his brain that was willing to make room for the impossible.

"How do I know? I've never had an experience like this. Have you two?" But yes, she had. She saw the vision again with the light coming near her on that hill overlooking the ocean where Ted, she thought it had to be him, streamed in on a light beam to rescue her. *I don't need to be rescued,* she told herself. *Or do I? Don't we all?*

"Don't forget to include George. He's part of your vision, if I'm not mistaken. On that strange note, I've got to go prepare for a really big week ahead." Jessie walked out the door into the dark night with Joe by her side. Though it was one of the safer neighborhoods in Naperville, Joe wanted to make sure she got into her car without any mishaps.

"Hey Jessie, you forgot your keys. I'll bring them to you."

When she ran into the kitchen, where Jessie left her keys, Beethoven's Ninth startled the daylights out of her. She reached for both the keys and her phone.

"Excuse me, Louise. I'm sorry to intrude." It was Jacob, Ted's son.

"How nice to hear your voice again. Is there a problem?"

"Not at all, I changed my mind about your meeting me at the art museum. Instead, I'm going to pick you up at your home. I know where you live and how to get there. I'll be there at 4:00 p.m. on Tuesday. Will that be okay with you?" Then there was complete silence. He was waiting to hear her answer.

"It's okay with me, but ..."

He interrupted her. "No buts. I want this visit to be as easy on you as I can make it. I'll see you Tuesday."

She placed the phone on the counter as Jessie's hand reached for her keys she dangled and clinked in her hands.

"Who was that? You look numb, transfixed, and could it be transformed?"

"That was Ted's son..."

"No, he's cancelled his trip. I knew it was too good to be true."

"Jessie, he's going to pick me up here Tuesday, at my home, here, right here." She pointed, twirled around, and ran into Jessie who caught her before she lost her balance.

"Easy does it, Louise. We're going to know what to do next as surely as I know tomorrow is my birthday."

"Jessie, as surely as I know tomorrow is your birthday, I could never forget it. Each of the steps we must take will come into being just as you did forty six years ago. Look how you've been revealed in all your individual and separate glory, as if God is creating you as we speak and search."

"Wow, what a fancy birthday wish. It's as if I'm being baptized and shown to the crowd. It makes me miss my mother. She always made a big deal about my birthday. I was baptized when I was one month old, as close to my birthday as possible."

"Jessie, you would have been baptized on Palm Sunday or Easter Sunday. You were a glorious gift to your church family and your actual family."

"I want to talk about my mother and how close I've been feeling to her lately. Maybe because it's my birthday or the time I was baptized. Maybe there's something to life going on after death. She's not here in a body form, but I feel her spirit."

"Can you describe her spirit to me?"

"It's not like she was when she was living in her body. She's not like that. I don't feel her emotions or her ups or downs, those sorts of reactions. I'd have to think about this some more before I can put words to what I feel coming from her, but I know it's my mother."

"Does she talk to you, Jessie?"

"I don't hear words, no, not words. It's more like I'm being moved by a gentle breeze toward an idea or thought I didn't think I had. She may be trying to get me to express some hidden notion, like a seed that needs to take root and grow into a mighty shoot."

"The Spirit of God blows like the wind, depending on what message God is speaking to us and how serious it is. Do you think your mother is just being your mother or do you think she has something urgent to tell you?"

"She loves me in ways I've never been loved, you know what I mean? Do you think she knows how much I miss her?"

"Yes, I do. I'm not sure they miss us. I do believe that our loved ones who have died, if we want to call it dying, can make efforts to comfort us so we can have room to grow into ourselves more completely."

"God is like a mother, a parent. Why wouldn't it be okay for our departed loved ones to continue to love us on some level?"

"Hence, my soul mate who made the move first to love me from wherever he is. I was not thinking about him though I missed him in my heart and soul where no one could see my grief and sorrow."

"Could it be that our departed loved ones can miss us and want to get a reaction or help from us?"

"It's hard to tell whether they want to help us or need help from us. I think it's a reaction from them to us and vice versa. I just thought of this, in this way then they become us and we become them."

"Brilliant, Louise. We have proven there is no death in that theorem you developed."

"Totally out of necessity and from missing a loved one we become them, they become us, and we become better humans whose spirits are able to merge with theirs and God's or what you might want to call the cosmic, corporate spirit."

"I'd still like to be able to see my mom, feast my eyes on her smile, and bask in her warmth."

"The more our spirits grow stronger and healthier in us the less we will miss the physical elements."

"That's not going to happen to me anytime soon, Louise. My appetites are erratic. Just when I think I have one under control like my food appetite then some other appetite runs out of control, like my anger over dumb drivers."

"To gain perfection and be able to help our spirits reach their potential while we're here on earth, we have to tame our appetites and our emotions then, I heard someone say this yesterday, miracles occur.

"I can't get over my desire to see my mother. Every day is a struggle to get my grief under control. I think I will live this way the rest of my life, Louise."

Louise had never seen her look so sad and forlorn, like an orphan during a war. "Jessie, here, read this paragraph in this book I'm reading. It might help both of us understand how time is timeless and how everything that ever was or will be is happening at the same time. That means that people who have died are still living sometime someplace."

"...J.M.E. McTaggart, in 1908, posited that human perception deceives us: time only feels like a forward moving, flow because of the limits of our minds, whereas time actually exists, as does space, with everything in existence simultaneously, even if one is not there anymore. The events of twenty

years earlier still exist, just as another country and its inhabitants exist even once you leave it. Block time (is how McTaggart termed it) was like turning backward in a novel, finding dear characters preserved, quipping and contriving as ever. Block time offered comfort to secular minds, for those who had no heaven in which to save vanished friends." (page 370, *The Rise & Fall of Great Powers* by Tom Rachman)

"Louise, what does that mean? Are we right in thinking that maybe there is no death? Somewhere in time and space my mother, your soul mate, and all the other people who have died from the beginning of time are just lingering, not sure where or what to do next?"

"What it says to me is that all of us, including Albert Einstein, want to know why we're here and where we go when we die. Death has been a major subject most of our history on this planet. I agree with Einstein's theories of space and time and how everything occurs at once. There is no past or future. Every form of life is present now."

"But we still can't see the people who have died or left us in body form."

"Unless we are able, we have the ability we haven't developed yet to see everything at once. Think about what that would do to us. We couldn't take how seeing everything that always has and always will exist would stimulate us, probably out of existence."

The door bell rang and interrupted their discussion that did not materialize their loved ones. Jessie suddenly realized she had to go, but she wanted to stay.

"Look who we have here. It's Joe with a big box. I wonder what's in the box, Joe?" Louise and Joe had planned a special birthday celebration for Jessie. Now she knew the reason he left early.

"Here, Jessie, open up this box. You're going to be so surprised. You'll never forget this birthday, not in a million, billion years!" Joe was proud of himself as he placed the box on Louise's dining room table. What Jessie had not noticed were the plates, utensils, presents, funny hats, and hooters on the table.

"Louise look, it's a train. Joe where'd you find it?" She was so excited she couldn't contain herself. The little girl came out the way it had when she was a child and her mother made a cake for her.

"Notice my dear, it has chocolate-nut frosting, your favorite, and it's not just a train, it's an old steam engine. I know you liked trains when you were a little girl and your mom and dad took you down to the train station to see the big old engines pull their cars through the station out into the country."

"I don't know what to say! I'm flabbergasted that anyone would go to the trouble of making my birthday so special. Are you saying you, Joe, made this cake?"

"Hey, I have lots of skills and cake baking is one of them. I only bake for special friends. The rest of the world has no clue how great I am."

"Do you think if we had that special vision we were talking about before Joe came, we could see all our relatives around this table who had celebrated our past birthdays with us?"

"Think of it as this being your one and only birthday that has lasted for an eternity."

"What in the name of God and God's angels are you talking about, Louise, that all our dead loved ones are still here but we don't have the skills and abilities to see them?"

"Something like that. We have some evolutionary steps to take before we can rejoin everyone who has every lived on this planet or will live on this planet."

"Won't it be a tad crowded when that happens?"

"I don't think we'll have the same appetites and desires we have now. Maybe we won't need to eat, sleep, buy clothes, drive cars, or fight with each other."

"What a wonderful birthday present to know that my mom is still here someplace and, Joe, your dad is too, and Louise, so is your soul mate. This is a big clue, but where do we start to look for them?"

"Clues are all over the place, my dear, dear friends!"

"Your vision is better than ours, we fear."

"No fear allowed on this hunt for the living who –have you thought of this – are in greater living shape than we are?"

"If they don't have to worry about stuff like appetites, violence, and everything bad that has ever happened to the people who have appeared on earth and have been replaced by us. You see, don't you, what a lot of worrying goes on among all of us just to continue breathing, eating, living, sleeping, buying, and avoiding harm and damage?"

"You're making me long for the time when we can shed this mortal coil like my soul mate Ted did. I think he got tired of all the details involved in living every second on this material plane."

"Not ready to leave this form yet, are you, Joe? Are you, Louise?"

"Depends on what other clues we find. They may entice us to change our form." Louise wasn't joking. She thought she'd find her soul mate and that he'd convince her it was time to leave.

Chapter 8

JSV Day

March 28, 2015 – More investigations into the French Alp crash that obliterated the German Wings plane and the passengers.

March 28, 1979 – Near Harrisburg, Pennsylvania, the Three Mile Island nuclear power plant accident occurred threatening a catastrophic nuclear meltdown.

All three friends, Louise, Jessie, and Joe and Louise's black cat George Oscar, woke to an excitement they hadn't known since they couldn't remember. It was similar to feeling like the world they knew was coming to an end.

Jacob, Ted's son, was going to drive to her house from Midway, a thirty-minute drive, and take her to dinner. Louise suggested a new restaurant that just opened about a mile from her townhome.

Joe called her to ask, "Didn't you tell me that Ted's middle name was Jonathan? Jacob is named after his father."

"Good memory, Joe. His middle name was Jacob, bless his soul." She wondered where his soul was and the reason she said it was Jonathan.

"Louise, things are going to change and not just a little, a huge amount equal to a world that hasn't been discovered. We should have a few moments of silent respect for the sacredness of the past and how it has helped us stay focused on the here and now, not easy to do in this world of many distractions."

"And, all the saints be praised, the future too has already been declared sacred by a force greater than we are." Times like this, when she had no idea what the future would bring, she realized how tiny humans were in the full scope of life in the cosmos. Her insides crinkled and cringed at the thought that would cause a less observant person to think they were having hunger pangs.

"I think we're going to need all the saints forevermore to protect us when we see what Jacob wants." Joe didn't know that he was prescribing the future without knowing the complete diagnosis and prognosis of the illness, if that is what you call the need for change they faced.

"Love, Joe, love is the answer. The kind God has for us will stand between us and any evil intention." She believed Jacob was coming on a love mission for his deceased father.

"Bless you, Louise." He meant it, then disconnected the call and drank his coffee in one gulp. "I hate coffee."

Louise waited in a silence that took her breath away.

She wanted to talk to her grandparents, Grandpa Jim and Grandma Isabel. What did they think about death and dying and giving up the love they have for each other? She wanted to know the answer to that question before she met with Jacob.

April 25, 2015 – The Nepal Earthquake wrecks Katmandu and kills thousands.

April 27, 2015 – Funeral service for Freddie Gray, whose spine was broken after an encounter with the Baltimore police.

April 27, 2015 – Riots break out in Baltimore after Freddie Gray's funeral, the worst burning and looting since the 1960's.

Grandpa and Grandma's love relationship

Grandpa Jim was on his way to visit Isabel, his wife, Louise's grandmother, in a facility not far from their home in Naperville. He waited to call Louise back after he parked his car in the parking lot not far from Isabel's wing. He didn't believe in driving and talking.

"How's my Pumpkin doing?" He had called her this name when she was a baby, later so had her father, John Irving, who was named after a relative of both families. Apparently, Louise's mom and dad were first cousins once-removed before they were married. Their mother's mothers were sisters. Everyone in the family thought that Louise and her brother might turn out to be idiots since their parents were such close relatives. They were proud of the fact that they had proven the skeptics wrong with their above average IQs. Their parents' love for each other had defied the naysayers and in the end had produced two children who cared deeply about life on earth and making it better.

"Grandfather," she always got his attention when she was so formal, "you and Grandmother, I know I'm being very formal here, are soul mates, right? At least, she's your true love."

"We were lucky to find each other and to still be so in love with each other after sixty-five years of marriage. We are always there for each other, through thick and thin, through good weather and bad." Jim Cappston was so handsome, lean and trim that Louise could not believe he was eighty-five years old. He didn't have a potbelly nor did he have to wear glasses. He told everyone that he came from good genes. His father, Louise's great grandfather, was one hundred and eight years old when he finally died. His wife, Jennie, died a year later when she was one hundred and nine. Jim would tell people who asked that diet and exercise do make a difference. "Don't drink or smoke. They will kill you quicker than you can imagine." He knew this was true after his son, John Irving, Louise's father died, smoking and drinking killed him in his sixties. He had performed his own intervention in his son's life after Louise was born. He told his son that if he didn't stop drinking and clean up his act, he would take care of his children himself. His warning worked for about six months then he was back drinking and smoking before the year's end.

Louise could almost read her grandfather's thoughts. "Dad and Mom didn't have the kind of relationship you and grandmother have. You are one with each other's thoughts and actions, right?" If only her parents had had that kind of love, maybe her father wouldn't have died too soon from drinking too much and she knew it had to be true that she and Stan would be married today and enjoying their children together if they hadn't had such a fragmented love.

"It goes deeper than that, Pumpkin. It's like we've always known each other, not just in this lifetime and I've never been one to believe we've lived in other lifetimes. Now I can say to you how else can you account for two people, your grandmother and me, who instantly fell in love and have always been kind and gentle with each other? 'Don't I know you,' we said to each other at the same instant. I know you're thinking if only your parents and you and Stan could have had this kind of love you'd be free of regrets you have today."

"Grandfather, that's it. It has to be. You knew each other before in another time, in another life. You knew how to love and what you learned could not be abused or taken for granted. How else is it possible to love each other the way you do without harsh criticism or in some cases, violence and abuse either toward others or yourself?"

"Some of us have been able to tap into this indestructible love that is more important to share than it is to deny or destroy it because of our own insecurities." He was a man of deep thought who never said a word until he was convinced he believed all the words that came before and after his first word.

"Which means, Grandfather, excuse me for being so formal, that when you or Grandmother dies, you will not stop loving one another. Your love won't die, so why should you have to die? What do you think? Does the depth of your love provide you with another form of life we can't identify while we live in this form?"

"I have to be honest with you. I've been concerned about what will happen if I should die before Isabel does. What will happen to her? Will the love sustain her? The only way I can answer this question is after I leave this body."

"Grandfather, I have this feeling that you won't ever leave her though your body may wither and die. Don't ask me how I know that. I thought you might know about the inner workings of love and its permanent nature."

"What is prompting your questions? Have you found love again or are you thinking about trying to find someone who will truly love you, someone who deserves you?" Jim was always more concerned about others than he was himself. For him to ruminate about love, Isabel, and his own fears was making him uncomfortable about his own self-concerns.

"Oh, gosh, Gramps," she felt like a little girl again who could trust her Gramps with the biggest secret in the world, "I don't know where to begin to tell you how this love I feel for this person started and where it is now." Louise was stumped on how to tell her grandfather that she was trying to find a dead guy she still loved and thought she'd see again soon.

"Start at the beginning, where'd you meet this guy? Tell me about him." All phases of himself were adjusted to the here and now. He was listening to words and emotions.

Louise told him she met this mysterious person by accident on a trip with Jessie. She had no intention of finding love but she found it the instant they met. She couldn't help how her heart took a major tumble into a love she told her grandfather she didn't believe would ever end.

"What's more, Gramps, I think I've always loved him. When I saw him, I thought I had already known him but didn't know where or how. You know what I mean, don't you?" Louise thought how fortunate she was to have a grandfather who loved her in spite of her doubts and fears.

"And now he's dead, Louise?" He was being formal. There is such a fine line between how easy we feel around the people we love and we think love us that anything can change the dynamics, especially when life and death, love and hate are involved in one conversation.

"He died eight years ago and I believe he is trying to contact me! In this case through his son, not a medium somewhere. I'm not into that sort of crazy stuff, Gramps."

"I know you better than that. You would put yourself at risk for love if it has the substance this love seems to have. Our faith, yours and mine, is too strong in the twenty centuries-long search for Jesus who refused to stay dead! We believe that one day he'll come back to us from the dead. He can't be the only living soul who has come back from the dead for a loved one."

"He was resurrected into a different life form. We have to agree with that major premise of our faith. Since I believe that faith and love work together to reconstruct a life in and beyond this life, why couldn't it be possible that this man I fell in love with quite by accident is still here but in a different form?" She knew her grandfather couldn't describe what happens after death, but he was an expert about how and when to sacrifice his love and life for others.

"And that he either wants you to help him out of a bind or he's here to help you. You see, I know that love is always trying to find solutions to problems we don't think have solutions on this plane," Gramps said this without hesitation. Louise thought that was the result of his wife's total healing from Alzheimer's that came about largely because of his love and belief in her healing.

"Gramps, did you help her heal with your love?" This should have been a statement but it came out as a question. Louise didn't have a chance to alter the emphasis.

"Absolutely! My love and the love God filtered through me into her and from her into me penetrated the walls of this awful disease and crumbled them, just like the walls of Jericho. Love always has to work both ways for it to edify us and move us onto another level of existence."

"Where are you now, Gramps?" He was more her father than her grandfather. Her father had died when she was in her thirties. Her other grandfather, her mom's dad, had died when her mother was a teenager. What a joy to have a father and grandfather in one person, a wonderful blend of two different kinds of love that grow stronger the more it encounters the need for love. How strong and defiant it needs to be, like now when Louise was fighting for her soul mate that may be a mirage. "Gramps, are you saying that our faith is based on searching for a dead guy who won't stay dead?" Louise was thinking that death encourages people whose loved one has died to never stop searching for proof of life.

"Louise, love as deep as I have for your grandmother and you have for your soul mate has to require of us that we believe in the everlasting quality of life and love. That we will look up one day and there our loved one will be with a new body, sparkling new, free of illness, regret, worry, violence, or abuse."

"You mean I can search for him as I am now and I'll find him? Where, Gramps, where?" That was Louise's major question, where is he now if not in the coffin in some cemetery plot?

"Ah, now you are asking a question I can't answer. Isabel, my true love, my soul mate, has not died yet from this plane. I can reassure you that there is a greater plan than we can fathom with our physical senses when we search for that love and where that search will lead us."

"When I learned that my soul mate, Ted, had died, I can't tell you how I ached inside, as if I didn't want to believe in a life beyond this one. My own mind convinced me that his life was over forever. My heart broke into a million pieces that I found impossible to put back together again, like Humpty Dumpty falling off that wall years and years ago."

"I know what you mean. When I think about Isabel dying, my heart lurches out of control and it takes me with it into that territory where I'm easily convinced I'll never see her again. Then something, probably love, echoes in my heart allowing all those jagged pieces of myself to reunite in a great act of creative love."

"Gramps, love doesn't allow life itself to disintegrate like dust in a dust storm, blown millions of miles from its center. Grandmother will never stop orbiting around your center like an atom that is able to reform you."

"Is that what you are feeling from your soul mate?" He was genuinely interested, which amazed Louise.

"Yes, he's telling me that even in death love survives and love has a purpose even in the face of impossible odds."

"What is love's purpose?" He was thinking that they had spent most of their lives searching for an answer to their faith and wanting it to be in the person of Jesus Christ. Now they had to search for a deeper meaning of their love for their soul mates or for the people they love with our whole hearts, minds, and souls, and this love has to include God?

"God's love never ends and neither do we as human beings, though we change form, or do we? Is there a time when love will be so powerful and mighty that it will enable us to overcome death? Is this what my soul mate has accomplished? If we were able to allow love to clear up our vision, could we see him here with us?" This was the most important question of the century, Louise was convinced. If humans can survive death, like the Egyptians tried to do with their pyramids and supplies they piled around the dead body, what would humans be capable of doing?

"Yes, I think that's where we're headed in this stage of our lives. I've never talked about this with anyone because most people aren't ready to think like this."

"I don't know if I agree with you. I think more people are more ready than you think for this next phase of our evolution. It's getting harder and harder to live on this material plane."

"You mean that things don't satisfy us the way they did when we first discovered we could master the material elements? Yes, I think you are right. Death is the major obstacle to this leap we must make beyond the material. Love and faith combine to make the fuel that will jettison us into another realm."

"I could listen to you all day, Gramps. Where do we go from here? Will you help me find my soul mate, living or dead?"

"Could be he's already tried to contact me. After all, we're all on the same wavelength or love channel. Let me see if I can calm the waters between you two."

"Are we in any kind of danger if we try to get too close to that channel?"

"Not if we keep the love of Jesus Christ close to us. To say it a better way, if we stay close to Jesus and his love. He and that love will protect us forever and take us where we need to go. Your grandmother and I have always believed our love came from God and would return to God. In the meantime, there is that constant circulation of God's love that always keeps us safe and secure in the perimeters love creates."

"Does that mean you can travel anywhere and at any time to any place?"

"If you mean that you could find your soul mate centuries ago like I have your grandmother, then yes, you are never separated from that love."

"Eureka, Gramps, that means you will find her even after she dies or you die."

"I am hoping we will die at the same time. I've heard of that happening."

"But, I don't want you to ever leave me, not for years and years." She had spoken as a little child afraid to be left alone in a strange place.

"You still have a lot to learn about the nature of love and death, but I believe you are on the right path and that your love for your soul mate will keep you from falling into a bramble bush."

"Grandfather, how did you know about my bramble bush experience?" She was shocked beyond belief.

"There are some things I don't know how I know them. I trust what I say is appropriate or I wouldn't say it. I must have picked up some of your thoughts. That is also the nature of love that with it we learn more about the people we love, with or without words."

"My vision is clearing. Let me say it this way, even in death that love is with us teaching us more about love and life. Here's another question Gramps, will that love you feel for your wife, my grandmother, grow stronger in death?"

"Good question. I don't think there is any doubt that our love will be stronger and require a different kind of sacrifice to be made for it after death. The one that your soul mate is making for your love now may be greater than any sacrifice anyone has made on this earth."

"Even the death of Jesus on the cross?"

"He suffered great physical pain hanging on that cross, one can't doubt that. The kind of pain your soul mate is having, notice I said 'is having', can't be defined the same way we think of our pain here on earth."

"Surely then we don't have words for what he is going through now as he tries to contact me."

"Especially if you are not listening with your whole heart, mind, soul, and spirit."

"How often did Jesus try to get his followers to listen with their whole being, not with one part of it that changes with the wind or the tide. I can relate. I want all the parts of me to be united within and outside of me. I'm not sure how to get agreement with all the parts of me."

"I'll see if I can give you spiritual encouragement, the kind that comes from my love that extends out beyond who you see that I am."

"I'm humbled by your wisdom, Gramps. I didn't realize you knew so much that has nothing to do with book knowledge, though you're smart in that realm also." He had been a professor in math at a university in Chicago before he gave that up and became a farmer.

"The love your grandmother and I share made me smart on that invisible part of me because I realized that she knew more than I did. She had greater spiritual depth than I did. When I asked her to come closer to me in my spirit and admitted I didn't think I knew everything like some men want their women to think, I could not believe how she opened up to me. Her love gave me courage to open up like a sunflower, without my fears intervening."

"No one I know has that kind of love. Everyone is so defensive and competitive. They are afraid that if they share too much they won't have enough left for themselves. You are saying the more you give of that love the more you have to give?"

"Yes, you've always known that. Your loving actions have proven you know more about love than you think you know. When you find that God kind of love you just know that it won't end when you die. Something assures you, the very nature of love, that you will not have loved in vain. Do you think your soul mate thinks he has loved you in vain?"

"Gramps, I don't know the answer to that question. Does it occur to you that we are about to learn more about love and if it really does exist in death and if it needs justification?"

"One day, I'll tell you about the experience your grandmother and I had when we took a trip to the island close to England, where our family came from, and who we met there that convinced us that life, love, and faith overcome death."

"That's a whole other story, right Gramps?" Louise knew that it was part of the history of love that was about to convince her that her soul mate had never died and that his love for her was going to transport her to a new way of living, loving, and having faith.

April 28, 2015 – Baltimore is cleaning up after a night of rioting by teenagers who don't believe anyone cares about their wants and needs.

Chapter 9

Your Face is Familiar

March 29 and 30, 2015 – Now we know that the co-pilot intended to murder 149 innocent souls when he crashed into the French Alps. No one can answer how this young pilot could do such a horrible thing.

March 29, 1979 – In the U.S. Congress, the House Select Committee on Assassinations released its final report regarding the killings of John F. Kennedy, Martin Luther King, and Robert Kennedy.

March 30, 1981 – Newly elected President Ronald Reagan was shot in the chest while walking toward his limousine in Washington D.C. He joked later, "I should have ducked."

March 30, 1853 – Vincent Van Gogh was born in Groot Zundert, Holland. During his short career of ten years, he produced over 800 oils and 700 drawings, but sold only one during his lifetime. In 1987, the sale of his painting *Irises* sold for $53.9 million, the highest price ever paid for a work of art up to that time. He committed suicide in 1890 by gunshot after long bouts of depression.

At 3:45 p.m. George Oscar sidled up to the front door, sniffed, and gazed around and up while his tall wagged fast and in a circle. He growled and muttered as only he could, then he walked back to his favorite chair, changed his mind, and ran up the stairs into her room where he found refuge under her pillows. Louise never knew cats grumbled and growled as much as George did. This was a warning. He was telling her to get prepared, something big is about to happen.

She took extra time to bring out her best features that had been comfortable hiding behind the scenes. Her father told her mother when she was young, innocent, and ignorant of those fine features, that she had a natural beauty he didn't want to see hidden under too much makeup. Her blue eyes, light skin, and her lips she emphasized with a light shade of coral lipstick. She didn't use any other makeup. She was short, lean, and well-shaped for an aging woman. She lifted light weights and swam everyday to increase muscle tone and encourage good health.

Ted's face flashed in front of her after George the cat walked by her looking a bit flustered. She saw his beautiful bluish-green eyes that transported her to a tropical island where she remembered imaginary gentle breezes made their days together peaceful and serene. She was no longer concerned about her appearance or what Jacob would think or why Jacob was coming to see her.

She walked toward the door the second the doorbell rang like something mysterious had drawn her there before the bell rang. She shook herself to this dimension and opened the door with a combination of fear, joy, and anticipation.

"Please come in...Jacob." He had his father's face. She asked him, "Is this a dream?

"No, I thought it was before I rang your doorbell. Then I woke up to the real world that is thousands of miles from mine. Where am I, can you tell me? Oh, I know on the physical plane where I am. I haven't lost my mind. You're not at all what I expected."

She said this with the ease of a master in matters of the soul, "You look so much like your father, Jacob, which makes me know he had you come here for an important reason."

"May I call you Louise? It's urgent or I wouldn't have come here to disrupt your life and mine."

Suddenly they both lost their appetite. Earthly needs evacuated as if afraid of the impending clash of worlds this evening in a suburb of Chicago on planet Earth somewhere in the Milky Way Galaxy.

"I believe my father is here with us. God help me for saying this, but I think he is. I am ordinarily a grounded person who runs the business Dad started with a cool head and hard logic."

"You don't need to prove yourself to me, Jacob." They were standing in the hallway by the front door, staring at each other as if they had dropped in from separate planets. "Let's sit, shall we? Before we become cemented to the spot, like Lot's wife when she looked back at something she wasn't suppose to see and was turned to salt."

"Can I get you something to drink? How about I fix you a salad?" She wasn't hungry for earthly food. She could be a high lama whose essential nutrient was rays from the sun while sitting atop a mountain, preferably in the Himalayas. She felt comfortable being in Jacob's company. He carried Ted's genes in his body and Ted's light in his soul. Light is light however, not the light she saw in him.

Jacob was thinking the same thing about Louise. He had not yet related it to the light that he didn't know was shining out from his being. He could deduce later that it wasn't of the same nature as the light Louise turned on in the kitchen after light left the earth and was replaced by darkness.

"I'll help you. I'm pretty good at fixing one of the best salads in California." He ran six miles twice a week and worked out the other five days in his own gym. His skin was a beautiful shade of brown. He knew when to get in out of the sun.

When they sat down at the dining room table, used several times a month by Louise and her friends and talked until 11:30 p.m. Louise's phone played Beethoven's Ninth.

"Beethoven Ninth, Dad's favorite."

Louise didn't know that.

Jake, for short, could tell something was wrong on the other end of the conversation. He remained riveted on Louise and the expressions on her face.

"It's my son Kevin's son Michael, my grandson. He's got some medical problems that need immediate attention. He'd like me to come as quickly as I can." Before she could think of what to do next, Jake told her he'd fly her to Boston where her son and his family lived. "I can't ask you to do that. I'll make reservations on the next flight out."

"Which will be mine, I won't take no for an answer."

Louise could see firm resolve written all over his body. He knew he had to act fast for her or she'd take too much time getting to Boston.

"You win. I'll get ready and we'll be on our way. I have to tell my friends where I'll be. Joe, a lifelong friend, will take care of George, the nervy black cat whose eyes have bored a hole in your soul."

Joe wished her well and told her not to worry, he'd take good care of George. "We are like brothers," he affirmed, "George and I."

The end of April 2015 – There are several areas of clean-up after major disasters, Nepal and Baltimore, Maryland on opposite sides of the world. This proves that we are all united in our efforts to keep life from falling apart and slipping into oblivion.

When Louise left the house with Jacob, she knew that George Oscar was buried under her pillows. She hoped she had remembered to tell Joe where to find him if he didn't appear when he entered the house. She decided that she would only use her energies to be concerned about her grandson, Michael. She was already talking to God about his healing and wondered if Ted were having an influence on the outcome.

"Your grandson will be okay, Louise. I know this from a source I can't identify: God, my Dad, or my own intuition which I rarely use."

"Tell me more about your father and what led to his death. I know you said he wasn't ill but that he seemed to have an appointment he couldn't keep unless he died. There had to be more to the story of his life than that he decided he had to leave and couldn't think of a better way to exit life than to die."

"He never got over the death of my brother and how he took his life. Dad threw himself into his work and made even more money than he could use in ten lifetimes as a way to escape his pain. Oh, God, Louise, I didn't try to help him with his pain."

"Don't you think it was because your pain was greater than you could manage?"

"I was supposed to be strong for everyone. Dad didn't say this to me, but I knew he expected me to not show my emotions so I didn't."

"He wasn't being cruel. You know that I hope, Jacob. He was asking you to help him be stronger. He couldn't have done it without your strength. In many ways, you are like him underneath the facade you've hidden behind. All of us have one."

"I've never talked about any of this with another living soul until now. Is this why I'm here with you?"

"In case we never find your father in a corner of life that hasn't revealed itself yet, I believe your well being is paramount and so is mine. He left us way too early."

They were quiet. Each contemplated what he, Jacob's father and Louise's soul mate, meant to them.

He whispered to her, "I want him to be alive somewhere. I think he is, but I can't see him. My eyes can't adjust to this other shade or level of life."

"You're way ahead of most people when you realize that your vision needs to clear before you can see what your father means to you. Just yesterday my grandfather and I were talking about this special kind of seeing God has given us. It's there, Jacob. I know it is. We have to grow into it or it has to adjust to our mis-views until we can see the way things really are."

"Does that mean Dad is here with us? I need that to be true more than I've ever needed anything else in my life. Nothing has seemed as important as knowing that life doesn't end with death."

"We are both searching for the same answer. I didn't know I could miss someone as much as I miss your father. I've lost many people I've loved with my whole heart, but I've been able to adjust to their absence in my life much better. What that means I think we will discover together. We can't do this alone."

"I admit that a large part of me that changed the instant I saw you and knew that you would have some answers I need, though I don't have the right questions yet."

"The first one is, is your father alive and will our way of seeing allow us to see him?"

"That means, Louise, Dad expects both of us to change in ways that will test us to the limit and I'm not sure I have the wherewithal to endure the pain it's going to cause."

"On the contrary Jacob, this change we are already going through will give us the greatest pleasure known to human beings."

"The greatest pleasure I've had was when my son, Edward was born. I could see he was a tiny representative, a culmination of all the people who had ever lived and died in my family. He made sense of my life and created in me a whole person who began to know my real purpose in the life of the whole universe. Then my father died and my joy flew south forever."

"The kind of joy we're seeking now will never leave us. Call it true fulfillment, joy everlasting. Tell me more about your son."

"He's not just an extension of a family time line, he's a blend of people I loved before he was born like my grandmother, Julia, who loved horses and taught me to ride when I was five years old. She had a beauty that startled the horses when she approached them. I think they thought she belonged to them. Her jet black hair shone brighter than their brushed coats and her eyes were able to pierce the hearts of the hardest soul and tame the spirit of a wild horse. My son loved her instantly and learned from her to love not only horses but all animals. She taught him how to grow plants and how to call them by their right names."

"Is Julia your father's mother?"

"Yes, Dad was her shadow. Consequently, they both knew each other's thoughts before they could express them. I think Dad thought everyone had that ability. Then I didn't think anything of it. Talking with you and knowing how you two could communicate, I'm wondering if we all have that ability only we don't use it."

"What about Julia's husband, your father's father, what happened to him?"

"His name was John Sebastian..."

"My father's name was John Irving."

"My grandparents are both gone. They died minutes apart from each other. Would you say they were soul mates? Their love for each other was mysterious and ordinary, powerful and tender, neither one of them needed words to summon the other if there was trouble. Louise, they may have loved each other before they got here in this life. I can't imagine I'm talking like this."

"I'm not sure the world is ready for people who have loved

each other forever. It's a love that you have no control over. I learned that with your father. Its main function is not to do any harm, but to make life better on earth and between the people you are sent here to care for and love."

"Is that why you and my dad didn't live together or marry?"

"Basically yes, we didn't want to damage the people we loved and who loved us. It was more important that we recognize that the love we share, notice I said share, would never die. Why try to capture it? I think is what we decided without words."

"Yet, there was a hole in his heart that only you and your love for him could have filled. I wonder what it would have been like if you had been close to him when my brother took his life. You see, I don't think he ever healed from that terrible loss."

"I have deep regrets that I couldn't be there for him. Jacob, I don't believe he wanted to burden anyone with his doubts about the part he played in his death. I know enough about suicide and how loved ones believe they had something to do with it and could have stopped it."

"That's it! Yes. I could never penetrate the wall he erected after that day he found his body and thought he had to clean up the room where he shot himself. Something went dead in him."

"He's back, isn't he, Jacob, in his spirit? Could it be he is trying to clean up other complications he thinks he caused?"

"Is he asking us to help him? Can the dead do that, Louise?"

"Even in death, I think it is possible that we can make things right we left undone at the point of our death."

They were at Midway, Jacob parked his rental car and they both walked to his plane that was waiting for them outside the hangar where it had been serviced and filled with jet fuel for the trip to Boston. The skies were clear all the way to Logan, the weather report said.

You could see with the naked eye about forty-five hundred stars. *The same number of victims of the Nepal earthquake,* Louise was thinking with a great deal of remorse and sadness. *Things on earth are reflected in the heavens where our deeds, plights, and hopefully this flight are not forgotten forever.*

"Dad would have loved this sky!"

"Maybe he cleared it for us. I'm beginning to think we all have unusual powers we haven't begun to tap."

"Louise, I have a surprise for you. You know when we were talking about my son, Edward? He's the pilot of this plane. We hired him five years ago when he decided he'd rather work for us than one of the airlines."

"This is a long way from loving horses and cultivating plants. It's good to meet you, Edward."

He was strikingly handsome. He was a true blend of yesterday's despair and today's promise. Louise didn't know what that meant. He had Ted's greenish-blue eyes as did Jacob. She was surrounded by a tropical paradise.

"Good to meet you too, Louise. I know you were my grandfather's friend. I'm happy to fly you to Boston tonight so you can make sure your grandson is okay," He shook her hand and gave her a quick hug. "We'll get through this emergency together, Louise. I'll rejoin my co-pilot and between the two of us we'll fly you to Boston safely." At the door to the cockpit, he turned and said to Louise and Jacob, "On the way our here, I felt closer to grandfather than I did during the last several years of his life. Why that is true, I have no idea."

Jacob loved his son very much. Louise could see love bursting out all over him. What a sight to see. *Maybe we'll find out why all of us feel close to him on this spiritual odyssey.*

April 29, 2015 – There are massive peaceful protest marches in Baltimore, Washington, Boston, and New York City. People of all races, genders, and creeds are asking for a solution to police brutality and the great economic disparity among races in America.

It appears that we are all on a spiritual odyssey where we are demanding that everyone have a good life on this planet and that sooner rather than later, we will not tolerate one percent of the world's population to have all the wealth and advantages.

In Louise's mind she was asking for the spread of joy and love to those not happily dead.

Chapter 10

An Unexpected Destination— A Journey beyond what we know

March 30, 2015 – Authorities construct a road to the crash site in the Alps so the families of the victims of Flight 9525 can see the site for themselves and have closure and the terrain equipment can clear the wreckage and the bodies. Saudi forces surge against Iran backed Houthi rebel forces in Yemen.

Jake made arrangements with his team to take over in his absence. He had an emergency that was under control and he told them not to worry.

Louise was in good hands. She felt as secure as she did when her father took care of her when she was a child.

March 31, 2015 – Deadline day for a nuclear deal with Iran. The co-pilot of flight 9525 said to have suicidal tendencies.

March 31, 1991 - The Soviet Republic of Georgia, birthplace of Josef Stalin, voted to declare its independence from Soviet Russia after similar votes from Lithuania, Estonia, and Latvia. After the Georgia vote, Russians troops were dispatched from Moscow under a state of emergency.

March 31, 1732 – Franz Joseph Haydn was born in Rohrau, Austria. Considered the father of the symphony and the string quartet, his works include 107 symphonies, 50 divertimenti, 84 string quartets, 58 piano sonatas, and 13 masses. Based in Vienna, Mozart was his friend and Beethoven was a pupil.

Jake and Louise flew through the night to Boston to be with Louise's grandson, Michael. They could have slept, but they had to talk about the reason Jake came to see Louise.

"I told you that Dad spoke your name the night he died. I asked him to tell me who you were and he said that you were in his soul."

"Was he in the hospital? Where was he before he died?"

"This is the strange thing about his death. He didn't exhibit any symptoms. No one knew he was ill. He was sitting outside on his patio where he could see the stars in the sky. It was a crystal clear night, the kind of night Dad loved. He said he could see forever."

"You mean he wasn't sick?"

"No, he was saying he had a mission he had to finish but wouldn't say what it was. I think it had something to do with you, Louise, and maybe your grandson. I have no idea why I said that. The business world is more predictable."

"Not where your father is concerned, Jake. Can I call you Jake? He was not of this world. I think he came from a place where he is right now and I have no idea why I am saying this. I've been a well-grounded realist most of my life."

"I know what you're saying about Dad. He had this unusual ability to know what you were thinking before you did. Those eyes of his could bore a hole through you. Not with anger, though he could get angry, but with deep compassion and understanding. No other father I knew when I was a kid had his perception and understanding. At first I didn't like it that he was my father. He was too weird. Now I yearn to have him back. I miss him with every fiber in me."

"Jake, Jake, Jake, when I heard that he had died, I had the same kind of yearning. I've lost many significant people in my time and never have I had such an intense desire to resurrect the dead. Wait, we're in the midst of Holy Week. Easter is this weekend."

"I almost forgot. Do you think it is a coincident that Dad made himself known during this holy time?"

"Do you have a strong faith, Jake?" She never asked people this question unless she could see they were in deep trouble.

Though trouble was not the right word to describe where the two of them were and what their destination was. They wanted to know if life continued past death and if there were a place where they could find Ted, alive and well with a new body and a new life.

"My faith was built on my ancestors' faith. We are all Catholics. I know you are a retired Protestant minister. We don't have lady priests, as you know. I'm not use to sitting in the company of someone so distinguished."

"In my denomination, most members have lost their respect and reverence for ministers. We are rated below car salespeople."

"Ouch! I don't think that is justified where you're concerned. I see you as genuine and real and someone honestly involved in the lives of the people who put their trust in you."

Louise was beyond being flattered. *Jake doesn't flatter people,* she told herself. She didn't respond. It was more important to listen to him.

"If Dad had you in his heart and soul, as I think he did, then I know you are genuine and that I can trust you with my life too."

"There's more to this story than you're telling me. Isn't that right?" Chills or tingles, she couldn't tell which, played a strange melody up and down her spine.

"I think so. I'm transporting myself from a world I'm accustomed to living in to this one I am sharing with you. We are being whisked through the sky in one of the fastest modes of transportation to an unplanned destiny. I believe it is part of Dad's plan."

"But it's not your plan, is it?"

"Not in a million years, Louise. I think my father is behind this. My thoughts and my feelings are that his intentions are to make sure all of your needs are well taken care of."

"That is beyond any of my expectations. I've been able to take care of myself since my mom and dad prepared me to be on my own."

"When was that? My guess is you were making your own decisions when you were in high school."

"Somewhere around that time I decided I'd be a minister against my parents' wishes. No matter how hard they tried to sway me, I held my course."

"Dad was always there watching and waiting but he never interfered with my decisions unless he thought I'd be in danger of ruining my future."

"He was the best protector alive on this planet. You were in excellent hands. I can see that you benefitted from his guidance."

"I miss him! I've already said that. I'd like to have him back."

"It makes me think of all the people who call themselves Christians and how they worship a live Savior. I never thought of it this way, but it occurs to me that they are after the same knowledge we are."

"Yes, that the life of our loved ones continues on another plane, one that we can't see. Dad is telling me, when I listen with everything I have, that that dimension is within plain sight."

"Yes, exactly what I couldn't put into words. You could have preached a powerful sermon."

"Dad cautioned me to listen more than talk. You'll learn more that way. I had to speak my mind to you. I knew you would listen with your heart if I interpreted my father correctly about you."

"I'm not too good to be true. I'm fallible, weak, and unable to make up my mind when life needs to take a harmless turn. What I'm good at doing is functioning at an A+ level when a crisis comes into the lives of the people who expect me to care for them."

"This is a harmful turn of events? Is that what you're saying?" His expression was penetrating. His eyes were perplexed.

"You see what I mean. There are times I have to be more precise in how I express myself."

"When a crisis comes, it requires that we take more time to form our opinions and the way we articulate them. I learned that if we get sloppy or are rushed into saying something, anything, we can lead people astray."

"What else, Louise? What are you really saying?"

"That we are on a journey to find your father and he won't be where we expect him to be. Does that sum up your thinking, too?" She was ringing her hands.

He was pacing. When he turned around, he walked toward her, took her hands, lifted her to her feet, and hugged her. "I bet you haven't been hugged with a Silva-Ventura hug lately. Thank you for being here for me."

When she sat down, her cells had altered and her thinking was rearranged. "You are more like your father than you think. You have his molten warmth that makes you see things surrounded by light and love. You don't mean to do that but he did."

"Where do you think we'll find him?"

"I have no clue. There are no traces of him."

"On the contrary, I have a box he left for me to go through with you on this day. He wrote this date down, today's date, on the box. Isn't that incredible? How did he know this date would be so important to us? Louise, do you know?"

"No, I do not know but together we will find out. There will be more clues. Can I see the box?"

The engines of the brand new Gulfstream eight-passenger jet whizzed through the night with an assurance and ease that settled their nerves and gave them comfort. It was a light and graceful flight compared to a heavy commercial jet flight. She was grateful to Jacob that he insisted he fly her to Boston and back.

"By the way, Jacob, thank you for insisting on flying me to my grandson's bedside. One could get use to flying this way everywhere."

"You mean where Dad might be hanging out?"

"We could fly on the wings of angels and land on his doorstep." Louise was certain this plane had the capability to fly to unknown parts of heaven and earth. "Jacob, this plane is a God-send!" She didn't know much about planes but this one had a spirit of its own.

"One of Dad's last wishes was that we replace the old, worn-out jet. He picked it out."

The Ninth played as they were about to change the subject to the box that Jacob brought for Louise to open his father had said he wanted her to have.

"Hey, Kevin, how's Michael doing? Can you believe it? That is just great!"

"Mom, he's going to be able to go home tomorrow. The doctors say it is a miracle he recovered so quickly. Maybe I've been wrong about prayer working because I know you've been praying for him. It will be great to see you, if only to celebrate Michael's quick recovery!"

"I can't wait to see Michael. I ask that you continue to believe that prayer works, but so do very good doctors and nurses and your own love for him!"

Their father had convinced both of them that there is no God and if there is, this God doesn't care about the human race. Why waste your energies on what most people use as a crutch?

For a long time, they believed their mother was a weak-willed person who couldn't think for herself.

After she told her son she loved him and his family very much, she disconnected the call and sat still too long with her head down.

"Louise, are you okay? We know that Michael is. What's going on inside you?"

"Just thinking about the long, hard battle to shutter my ex when he had brainwashed my sons into believing there is no God, that prayer doesn't work, and that anyone who believes in God is weak and uses religion as a crutch." She raised her head and realized that Edward and Jacob were concerned about her well-being.

"We both know a little bit about people who think believers are weird and weak. Toward the end of grandfather's life, his faith was stronger than it had ever been in his life. He read the Bible that he carried in his pocket of whatever he was wearing every day. His life revolved around his prayer time. He didn't care who saw him lower his head. We learned to respect his changed nature, but we tended to think he was getting senile." Edward had a challenge ahead of him. Louise could see that in how he spoke about his grandfather. He had a lot to learn about the spirit and the journeys it takes to find its truest fulfillment.

"Louise, how do I say this... I too thought Dad was losing it. That his mind was going, until I had that talk with him I told you about on the patio when you could see thousands and thousands of stars with the naked eye. I could *see* that Dad was clearer and deeper and more in touch with life than he had been most of his life, except after he met you."

"Don't you think that confused him, muddied the waters in his soul? I had the same experience. It has taken me years to recover from realizing that there is a love that never dies, that reconstructs you, and that stays with you until you have put yourself back together. Then it has the audacity to lead you into still, crystal-clear waters. My one son is beginning to see that maybe there is more to faith and love than meets the ordinary senses."

"Dad couldn't stick around long enough to share his new-found knowledge with us. Why do you think that's true, Louise?"

"I have wondered the same thing, Jacob. Why did he leave us at this time of our lives when we all needed him so much? Unless…" They were sitting on the edge of their seats, including Louise.

"Unless, why? Oh, there's something we have to learn he couldn't teach us while in his material body. No, that can't be, can it?"

"Dad, you are sounding a little crazy. What are you getting at? That grandfather had to die for a reason we have to discover on our own?"

"What we are going to try to prove is that death does not kill love, faith, or truest intentions. I don't know where I'm getting this string of words."

"Fiber optics," Louise said. "Your words are encased in light. As your understanding increases, the circuit will grow stronger and the light will lead us to the answer we all need to know." Louise had no idea what she was saying. "The word grows and as it grows it serves us in our present situation until we have agreed to allow the word to increase our heart or love capacity which will increase our faith exponentially."

"Now, you are talking like Dad was before he died. Hey, I forgot about the box Dad wants you to have. Maybe there are some answers or directions in it."

"What box, Dad?" Edward was mystified, just like her sons would be.

April 28, 2015 – Community leaders form a line, link arms, and put themselves between the protesters and police in Baltimore. Their message is loud and clear, in case you've lost your way home, we'll show you the way. They were seen steering and ushering heedless young people toward home and out of harm's way.

Louise thought that this is what we are all doing, trying to find our way home without causing needless harm to ourselves, to others, and to the planet that takes care of us. Teilhard de Chardin, a Jesuit Priest born in 1881, coined a term "the Omega Point" where one day we'll all come together in a unified whole. When we do, we won't need to inflict pain, endure pain, or cause pain to the planet. It will be like we've all learned that we've always been one on a spiritual level where the material body has been needed, but we won't need to rely on all the emotions it emits as much or at all once we arrive at the Omega Point.

"One last thought, gentlemen, your father/grandfather may have reached that resolution point in the universe. There he was called to release some of his complexities that were causing him undue pain and suffering. He shed that body of outdated thinking and didn't know how to transcend it without dying. I know this doesn't make much sense to you and it doesn't to me. I'm just mouthing the words and hoping that we will gain a greater understanding as we travel toward an answer on this, I'll call it a spiritual odyssey."

"Amen?" Edward still wasn't sure about God, prayer, or anything spiritual but he trusted his father and this stranger named Louise.

"We'll open the box on the way back from Boston. Edward said we'll land at Boston/Logan in twenty minutes. It's time to celebrate. We can stay the night if you want, Louise."

"No, I think I'd be in the way of his final release. Instead let's verify that this recovery is for real."

"I still think Dad had something to do with this miracle. Oops, Dad, God, and all of us."

Chapter 11

Things Work Out!

Before they landed at Logan in Boston, Louise thought of the movie, *Contact,* based on Carl Sagan's novel of the same name that he wrote with his wife, Anne Druyan. Jodie Foster played a radio astronomer who worked for SETI (Search for Extraterrestrial Intelligence). In a dramatic scene, she thinks she finds her father, who died when she was a child, walking on a beach in outer space in the Vega galaxy. He sends her back to her pod that has crashed before it was jettisoned. It is certain no one believes that she was gone for eighteen hours and that she found her father living on another planet. Sagan and Druyan wanted us to believe he was an illusion.

Carl Sagan, astronomer, astrophysicist, astrobiologist, cosmologist, researcher into extraterrestrial life, and atheist said he wanted to, but couldn't, believe in an afterlife. His book, *Contact,* was a way to present the possibility that there could be an afterlife. Sagan made it clear that he hadn't proven it to himself even after all his research, observation, and his T.V. series, *Cosmos.*

"Louise, I'll get the car I reserved and will meet you at the cab area in twenty minutes." He turned as he walked away and said, "Do you think we are delusional?"

"No, I don't. I think God is moving us in a direction that will benefit many people and my grandson, Michael will be one of them." Louise didn't believe that Jacob allowed himself to be distracted by doubts and fears very often. God knows we are trekking in a foreign realm but she was beginning to see wavering in the distance.

He waved as he left then turned around and told her, didn't ask her, to come with him. "I want to keep you close to me so neither one of us will be overcome by our doubts and fears."

"You must have heard me talking inside my head about whether you had any doubts and fears. I had decided that if you did, they were not scaring you like mine are scaring me. Where's Edward, what's he going to be doing? He's welcome to come with us."

"He's going to have dinner and then call home and the office. This trip has changed his center. I can tell. He's matured in seconds. Talking about doubts and fears, I think I saw many of them run for cover tonight."

"I think some of them jumped out of the plane and headed for parts unknown. Good riddance. Where we go from here is in God's control or I'd have greater doubts and fears. Remember Doubting Thomas and how he didn't believe Jesus had come back from the dead until he put his fingers in his wounds and felt the experience for himself?"

"Is that when we'll believe Dad is alive? When he proves it to us?"

"I think he trained us better than that!" For the first time, she could make sense of her encounter with Ted years ago when Jacob was a baby. *Was he an angel guide?* She had heard there were entities walking among us who looked human but were here to make our life easier.

"It's not too late to turn back, Louise."

"I don't think we need to be afraid. Jesus often told his disciples and followers not to be afraid more than three hundred times in the Bible. You don't need to be afraid!"

"Was God trying to indicate that there is no death, only the horror of death we bring upon ourselves? We talk ourselves into dying because we're afraid of living?"

"You're a good twenty-first century theologian. Your dad has forced you to come out of the Dark Ages with his urgings to see the light, especially the one he was carrying. I'm coming with you and I'm not kicking and screaming. I think this journey will be beyond comprehension. Our thoughts, ideas, and feelings will evolve as needed. Say it this way, they will help us climb to a new level of existence."

"Dad will be there, your dad too, and everyone who has died with a crowd of others who are ready to live as God expects us to live." He took a deep breath, smiled for the first time, and laughed a deep, rich baritone pitch that filled up the cosmos.

"You laugh like your father." She exhaled all the stale air from her lungs and felt the way she did when her grandfather pushed her high up on a swing in the city park until she'd squeal with delight. "Look, Grandpa, I'm as high as the trees! Higher and I'll be in heaven." He told her she was higher than the trees and not to be afraid. She never was.

They were moving toward heaven, if that meant they were not of this earth for the time being, as they walked toward the car Jacob had rented. He opened the door for her the way a gentleman would. He waited for her to get her foot inside before he shut the door. Suddenly, like a cold, threatening wind that blew down from on high, she thought of Stan, her ex-husband, who was too impatient to wait for her to be comfortable in any situation before he'd shut her out.

"Go away," she said aloud before Jacob opened the driver's door.

"You look like you've seen a ghost. Are you okay?"

"It's nothing. Well, I just had a vision of my ex-husband who was not very kind to me."

"There has to be a good reason for his 'ex' status."

"Your father was always kind to your mother, wasn't he?"

"Yes, he was. They were sweethearts in high school and got married when they were both twenty years old. I came along two years after my older brother who is no longer with us. They were very young parents."

"My parents had two children, my brother David and me. Dad taught him to be tough but Mom babied him, much to my father's chagrin. They had expectations for both of us, though their lives together were less than perfect."

"Dad and Mother never fought. That's the reason I found it hard to understand why he had you, Louise, in his life."

They were near the Boston Children's Hospital on Longwood Avenue, ranked higher in more specialties than any other children's hospital and one of the largest pediatric medical centers in the U.S. Louise knew Mike had received good care. She was sure he was mending.

"This is a big place. We know where we're going, don't you Louise?"

Louise had committed to memory the section he was in and his room number. She had called her son Kevin before they began their descent into Logan. He again affirmed that he had recovered, that it was a miracle and he thanked her again for her prayers. His kidneys were going to recover from the serious infection that nearly killed him. He said this all in one breath then added, "Thanks for coming, Mom. I can't wait to see you." He was tender and grateful. Her other son, Kurt, held his feelings in check behind a soft heart.

"I'm bringing the son of a friend of mine with me who flew me here. Is that okay?"

"Absolutely, it is. I want to thank him for getting you here so quickly."

"I'm just happy I didn't have to stand in line at an airport or worry about pilots, landings, or anything other than getting here."

Outcomes can be revealed quickly, as in the case of her grandson's recovery, or they can take their time to come to fruition, if they ever do. There are people who always think life is queer and unpredictable. These are the people who find it hard to trust God's powers and their own.

The leader of the militant atheists who has many followers, Richard Dawkins quoted Haldane, an eighteenth century biologist, about how strange the universe is. "The universe is not only queerer than we suppose. It is queerer than we can suppose." Dawkins goes on to think for himself, "Could we, by training and practice, emancipate ourselves from Middle World (where he thinks we are now), tear off our black burka, and achieve some sort of intuitive – as well as just mathematical – understanding of the very small, the very large, and the very fast? I genuinely, don't know the answer," Dawkins says, "but I am thrilled to be alive at a time when humanity is pushing against the limits of understanding." Even better, he ends his book, *The God Delusion,* by saying "we may eventually discover that there are no limits." (p374.)

"You know, Jacob, we are ready to cross over into a new land where Dawkins is right. Don't get me wrong, I'm not a follower of his militant atheism, but there will be no limits and we will find answers to questions we are finding the courage to ask."

"Like, is my father living in another land closer to us than we think and that illnesses are phases we are going through until this new land appears and every malady we've ever or will have disappears."

For the first time, Louise could see he was open to new possibilities that might threaten his life-long positions.

"Look how quickly Michael got well when he had all his loved ones around him and he knew you were on your way."

"Love is definitely the key, but I think there is another word for it that gives us the ability to delve deeper into life's mysteries."

"Do you think my father knew the key?"

"I think he has the key, but I don't believe he's the only one who has it. We all have it. It's written into our DNA. We have to allow God or some higher force to remind us of who we are."

"All of who we are is written into our DNA, Louise?" Jacob was functioning as a committee with his whole heart, mind, and soul to prepare for what was ahead of them. The last thought he had before he leaned back into his chair outside Michael's room and fell asleep is that he was sure his father had something to do with Michael's quick recovery.

Louise nudged him awake to meet her son and Michael, who had walked bravely alongside his father. Jacob awoke with a startled look, but quickly masked it with a warm greeting.

"Great to meet you. Hey, you must be Michael! You look too healthy to be in a hospital."

They all liked each other instantly. Michael and Jacob never took their eyes off each other. Louise wondered to herself what the two of them saw in each other. Later, Jacob would tell her that there was something about Michael's eyes that fascinated him. They looked familiar.

"I told you I thought Dad had something to do with your grandson's recovery."

"Are you telling me that you saw your Dad in Michael?"

"Or the results of a visit he made before we got here."

Louise thought that God often sends angels to care for us in extreme circumstances. *Was Ted one of God's angels who was caring for a myriad of other souls on earth?*

Before they left the hospital to fly back to Chicago, Kevin told her that he thought her visit changed the course of Michael's recovery. "Things were not looking very good for him until somehow he knew, we all knew, you were on your way here. This is one of the best children's hospitals in the world, but the doctors were not sure they could get his infection under control. They were preparing us for the worst. Then, suddenly, the infection left his body and he was well again. In the blink of an eye he got well. Was it you? Was it prayer? Was it you, prayer, and God? Was it all of you who came on that plane with God's help and whoever else came along?"

Louise didn't try to answer all his questions. He didn't need proof that his son was going to be healthy and strong and happy again. "There are forces you can't see, none of us can, that have resources we can't imagine or fathom while we are in these bodies. In the next few minutes before we leave, I'm going to be happier than I've ever been in my life for this turn of events. Things do work out in the whole scheme of things, often when we just let them happen."

Kevin and Michael hugged her at the same time. Michael was powerfully strong for one so young. There was great healing energy flowing through him that he spread to her, his father, and to everyone around him. He had a light that no one could extinguish. Even his father saw it and was amazed. On the way out of the hospital, Jacob and Louise were walking on air as if they had conquered one of the greatest human foes.

"Louise, Dad was here. I know he was. He left that light I told you about in Michael."

"Jacob, I think we're on his trail. He's leaving us clues."

"This is the oddest treasure hunt I've ever been on. The clues are more precious than those we had to find on our previous mundane searches. This is a life and past-death search."

April 30, 2015 – Baltimore is still trying to bring calm to the city after major riots. The question is how to heal the disparity between the rich and the poor, between people who are greatly limited and those who consider that the sky's the limit.

Louise spent most of her life trying to heal rifts and bring people together in spite of their differences. We won't, she was sure, reach that Omega Point of de Chardin's unless everyone has equal advantages, no matter what gulf separates them. If we can bridge the gap between life and death and find Ted, the father, grandfather, and soul mate, then the world ought to be able to make sure those with limited access to necessary resources are able to move across and back and forth over that bridge the people with unlimited resources help them build. Louise was sure Ted was helping them find the resources to build the bridge across the valley between life and death.

Kevin walked them to their rental car and then hugged and said goodbye to his mother with tears in his eyes, "How is it that we gave you such a bad time about your faith, Mom? Forgive me." He closed the door like a gentleman and gave her time to be well-situated. He had learned from the mistakes of both his parents how to be gentle and kind in a world where violence was all too common.

Louise was saying to her inner-self, *at least we are beginning to know why there is so much violence. People are afraid of what they don't have and that they think they want with every ounce of their desires and courage.*

As they searched for Ted and found a ray of his light in Michael, she was certain that he would leave more evidence of his life, even in death.

Chapter 12

Pandora's Boxes
or the Secret of Life?

On the flight back to Chicago/Midway, Jacob asked her if she'd come to California to visit.

"Will you fly back with me?"

Louise answered, "No, I've got too many things to do here. George Oscar, I can't leave him." When Louise called Joe before she got on board, he told her that he and George had become best friends. She was relieved to know that he had come out of hiding in among her pillows.

"Bring George with us. There's room for him." He had it planned that he could find a home for Louise close to his family where he'd watch over her as she got older. It's what his father would want.

"Is this conversation a distraction meant to take my mind off the box you brought with you? It's still the date your dad wrote on the box, that's one of the main reasons I didn't want to stay overnight."

"No, it's to take my mind off the box. I have never opened it. I don't want there to be Pandora-like qualities inside it."

"Might be full of hope instead, Jake. Your father wouldn't try to trick us." She was sure he wouldn't, but she was also sure that what was in the box would change their lives in incomprehensible ways. She thought of how the life, death, and resurrection of Jesus Christ, that one act, changed the course of history. For some, it gave them great hope. For others, an outlook they refused to claim. They had a 'I'll do it myself' attitude. "Where's the box, Jake? Can we take it out and stare at it? Maybe it will talk to us or it could have magical qualities like the Ark of the Covenant had in the movie *Raiders of the Lost Ark*."

"Look how those powers zapped the Nazis in the movie."

"Pandora's box in reverse," Louise conjectured.

"It'll take back all the evil and illnesses. It's up to you. Do what you think is best for you and your family. The box is here, in the plane, in the coat closet over there." He pointed toward the closet by the exit door.

Neither of them moved a muscle. They were fixated on the closet door.

"If I were Superman I'd use my x-ray vision to penetrate the contents. Then, I'd use them to neutralize whatever is inside."

"You're assuming it will hurt us."

"Not hurt, challenge us, Jake. Fear of pain and the unknown are ever present in our responses to life's challenges."

"Okay, I'll get up, walk over, open the door, reach down,

grab – no, pick up—the box, and walk back to my chair and sit down. Let's hope I don't trip."

"Leave the box on the table here between our chairs before you sit down." She realized he was a methodical planner. He didn't want to make mistakes.

The box was staring at them. They weren't the ones staring. "Now, what do we do?"

"Open the box. Open it carefully. Don't rush."

"You do it, Louise. I could never open my big gift at Christmas. Dad would finally do it for me."

"Here goes. May God be with us, bless us, and protect us in Jesus' name." She automatically made the sign of the cross out toward the box.

"You're not Catholic, are you?"

"The cross belongs to all of us." Her hands were shaking as she opened the flaps, Ted didn't tape shut the box. Inside was a note written by Ted. She knew his handwriting well:

> *Love is the answer. It's the road we must take to travel from this world to the next. You'll never find me where you think I should be. Life is not a mystery. We have always thought it was. Know that my love is forever. Death won't separate us or destroy our love.*

At the bottom of the box was an old wooden box that was locked.

"Do you have the key, Jacob?"

"I don't." He patted everyone of his pockets in his jacket and pants, nothing.

"How about your keys you carry with you? Are they on a key ring? Wait Jacob, the key is taped to the bottom of the box. This is too easy. Here, you unlock it."

"Pandora's Box number two." His hands shook as he unlocked the box. "A key. Look, it's a key with another note."

Louise said, "This is not like your father to send us on a treasure hunt."

"Read the note, Louise. I've never been this riveted in my life. I've taken everything for granted. I see that now."

"We don't have time for confessions, Jacob." She was being facetious.

His handwriting:

> *The key will unlock material wealth, more than you've known in your lifetime, Louise. You know this better than I. I had to find out for myself what great wealth will do to your soul. I trust you will use this money I've left for you to help you find true joy. Money doesn't belong to us. Joy does. It fills our hearts and gives us true peace. They can't be bought or sold. You taught me that, Louise. I love you with my soul.*
>
> *Thank you forever. Ted.*

"That's definitely his signature, Jacob. He didn't date it, a habit of his. Sometimes he would, sometimes he wouldn't. This time he didn't."

"It had to be days before he died. Or have you thought of this, he left behind one of his bodies and went someplace else with a better body? That gives me the creeps. Forget what I said. I think the molecules in this plane rearranged themselves. The air smells sweet but not too sweet."

"The kind of power your father has could make you see other worlds that have always been here."

"What's in the second box?"

"I'm afraid to open it, Jake. It's going to change my life in ways I'm not ready to accept."

"More than he changed your life thirty years ago?"

"You've got a point. Having more money than I'll ever use could be convenient."

"However, and there's always a however, I think there must be a plan behind giving you this money."

"You mean, conditions?"

"No, I don't. I think it may help you find him where you were found by him at one juncture in your life when you were struggling."

When she opened the box she found a small cable clad in fiber. It glowed when she lifted it out of the box, a fiber optics cable.

"It's a light, Jake! He's left us his light, my guess is in case we forget that the light will lead us to the answers we are seeking about death, his death, the death of all our loved ones, and our own death."

"What's that black book, wait, two black books under where the cable was?"

"One is a bank book." He had deposited five million dollars in an account with her name on it in a bank in Fremont, California. She couldn't breathe. "It's too much, Jake. A couple of thousand dollars would be more than enough. You take the money."

"Dad knew that's how you'd react. He knew you didn't care about the material realm the way he did. There's a reason he had to earn more money than he'd know how to spend."

The second black book was his personal small, well-worn Bible.

"Dad carried that Bible with him in a pocket of whatever he was wearing, another thing I took for granted. Louise, he's marked some pages."

On the inside cover page, Ted had written, "This Bible and its contents have saved my soul."

"Good timing, Dad. This is Easter week, in case it's slipped our minds."

"Jacob, you take the Bible. It's yours now. He'd want you to have it."

"These passages might offer a clue as to why he's nudging us in a certain direction with his spirit."

"I think he'd want us to know that they provided saving grace, say love, for his spirit he learned would never die. That's when we met, when he was searching for the answers he found."

"I still think he overcame death, somehow, some way, Louise."

"The passages may have given him the directions he is trying to give us. I've preached the message of salvation to many of my members, but not with the idea that they could avoid dying in pain, suffering, grief, and sorrow."

"The message Dad believed was that there didn't need to be sadness and darkness and grief, sorrow, and all those emotions that scare us when someone we love dies or we are about to die."

"Yet, if you believe in the afterlife the way Jesus proved there is, it could be your father wanted to bypass or grow past the greatest heartache indigenous to living life on this planet: shedding our skin and being born into a new way of life."

"I used to think this life is all there is. When we die, the lights go out forever."

The plane was making its approach to Midway, Chicago. Louise urged Jacob to look up the passages his father had marked in his well-worn Bible. The marked passages were Psalm 114, Philippians 2:12-13, 2 Timothy 3:14-19, and 1 John chapters 4 and 5

"I will add Revelation 21. Dad had me read it to him the evening he died."

"Are you sure he was in no pain?"

"He wasn't, Louise. His eyes radiated a light that filled the room and would have frightened a normal person to death."

"You mean the kind of death people don't recover from?"

"I never thought of it that way, but Dad recovered from his death before he died. Does that make sense?"

"It's beginning to, Jacob."

Epilogue

Even in Death

Jacob asked Louise to come to California with him. "We can find a house with a swimming pool, guest rooms for your friends, and a big backyard you don't have to share with anyone."

It all sounded too good to be true. Louise told him, "Not now, I've got things to do here."

Within a year, Louise moved to California, where the drought wasn't as severe. Jacob had a home picked out close to his neighborhood where it was safe. He didn't want her to feel deserted or fearful.

They both never stopped looking for the man who died with light shining out of his eyes, Jacob's father and Louise's soul mate. They continued to search for clues as to his whereabouts, though they knew by common earthly standards he was dead and would never be seen or heard from again. What they learned was that love didn't cause death. Love travelled past death as a new person into another dimension.

Louise, Jacob, Joe, Jessie, and George Oscar, the very precocious cat, were convinced Ted, the father, the soul mate, and the friend came to visit them at times when they reached a dead end in their search for the meaning of life.

Louise remembered how her second husband conveyed a message to her moments after he took his last breath. He told her not to be afraid of dying.

"It's good," he told her.

She heard his words, saw the light shining from his eyes, a broad smile on his face, and a glorious joy that made up his new body. She told him not to tarry. Go, enjoy your new life and he did.

Ted, her soul mate and father of Jacob, did tarry. He needed to make sure his loved ones were protected from what he feared would try to destroy them. That didn't mean her second husband didn't care about her future. He thought he had provided well for her before he died in great pain. All he could think about was getting free of the pain.

What Bruce told her was there were guides that came when everyone else was asleep and taught him how to exit this life. He could describe them and that there were three of them who guided him through the last minutes of his life.

Death is another phase of life. We come into life through a channel and we leave through a channel. We are accompanied by one or more angels or guides who take us where we have to go. They make every effort to assuage our fears in case we would come into and go out of life with terrifying fears and awful impediments.

When someone doesn't go off into another world like her second husband did and they stay close like Ted has, the question then becomes is there more to life than we can see with our naked orbs, our own little worlds?

Sequel: Clad in Light:

Forever Connected